TOURIST TRAVEL TREATS
FOR
OREGON/NORTHERN CALIFORNIA
(State of Jefferson)

by Wynne Gibson

Illustrations by Charles Travers

JEFF

SONJA

Tourist Travel Treats Oregon/Northern California
by Wynne Gibson
Illustrations by Charles Travers

Published by Wynne Publishing Company
P.O. Box 4713, Medford, Oregon 97501

Printed by Klocker Printery, Medford, Oregon 97501

© 1983 by Lucille Langston
First Printing 1983

Library of Congress Cataloging in
Publication Data   83-90460
Langston, Lucille   1983
ISBN: 0-915715-01-5 Softcover
ISBN: 0-915715-00-7 Hardcover

ABOUT THE AUTHOR

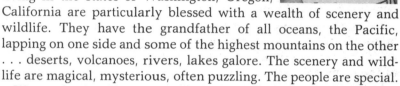

Lucille Langston, pseudonym **Wynne Gibson**, has written and published many human interest and travel articles over the past ten years. Putting a travel guide together is a new venture although she is a veteran traveler throughout the Orient, Europe, South Pacific, Canada, Mexico, and the western United States.

A Westerner, Wynne believes the people living in the states of Washington, Oregon, California are particularly blessed with a wealth of scenery and wildlife. They have the grandfather of all oceans, the Pacific, lapping on one side and some of the highest mountains on the other . . . deserts, volcanoes, rivers, lakes galore. The scenery and wildlife are magical, mysterious, often puzzling. The people are special.

Wynne begins *Tourist Travel Treats Oregon/Northern California,* by taking you on a personally guided seven day tour from Eureka, California, to Astoria, Oregon, and returns you via Klamath Falls, Oregon, Redding, California, over the Trinity Alps to Eureka. Each travel treat is experienced in your own limitless imagination.

Portland, Salem, Eugene, Roseburg, Grants Pass, Medford, Jacksonville, Ashland, Oregon, are only a few of the many cities and towns she guides you through in Oregon . . . you can even see Mare's Eggs in Ft. Klamath, Oregon. Tetrapods, Shasta Caverns, Samoa Cookhouse, Skunk Trains and the elusive Goose Lake await you in California.

Lecturer, traveler, writer, Wynne Gibson has been a long time member of the League of Women Voters, Professional Writer's Association, is a Laubach Literacy, Inc., tutor. She is married, has two sons, one daughter, four grandchildren. She golfs, swims, square dances, ballroom dances, bowls, and even "gives a shot" at a game of pool occasionally. Each year she makes it a point to learn something new . . . her philosophy: "we never stand still; we either go backward or forward."

Enjoy the family travel guide

Wynne

Tourist Travel Treats in Oregon/Northern California

A guide for fun, a guide for learning, a guide for the entire family as you travel about in the state of Oregon and northern California . . . part of which was originally known as the STATE OF JEFFERSON.

Tourist Travel Treats Oregon/Northern California gives you quick informative facts about particular places in a chatty and on a one-to-one basis, with particular emphasis on the young people's section. It is the author's opinion, in providing the young people's own index, maps, and line illustrated games, it is a first.

This travel guide does not attempt to compete with the many other beautifully done travel books of facts and photos. Type has been set for readability for young, senior, and in-between.

The line illustrations are sketched in the spirit of fun and no offense is intended to anyone or anything along the route of travel. Charles Travers is delightful in his amusing and cheerful portrayals of the many subjects.

In the first seven guides, the reader is toured personally up the California/Oregon coasts, down the Columbia River, through central Oregon and into northern California via Fairport, Alturas, Redding, Trinity Alps with the author acting as your guide for seven days.

Guide 8 cites the many resplendent, historical, and early Oregon beginnings in and around the city of Portland. Guide 9 covers the Portland to Eugene area, and Guide 10 takes us onto backroads and down I-5 from Eugene to Ashland and the Oregon border. Guide 11 is devoted entirely to young people.

Tourists become familiar with tetrapods, the Lake That Wasn't There, One-eyed Charlie, dune buggy rides, Samoa Cookhouse and the boarding-house-reach, Devil's Lake, Lacey's Dollhouse. Did you know the Sea Lion Caves house the rare Guillemot bird?

Tourist Travel Treats Oregon/Northern California contains over 100 jam-packed, fact-filled pages and fun illustrations. It is a book that every traveler through that area should carry with him.

FOREWARD

The human interest contacts with people, places, certain restaurants, motels, hotels, inns specifically mentioned in **Tourist Travel Treats for Oregon/Northern California** are noted from personal contact, personal observation, and personal research.

Prices are not quoted as Chambers of Commerce in almost every Oregon and California city or town have material they are willing to send free for the asking. They are up-to-date with current motel/restaurant prices in their areas.

The Red Lion/Thunderbird Inns are routinely mentioned throughout these GUIDES because the writer has found they provide quality in room appointments, service, food, and security in the areas traveled. The writer's comments by no means exclude many other fine motels, hotels, or inns from giving equal service.

Maps can be obtained at almost any gas station for precise routes, highway exit numbers, and indicated condition of federal, state, county roads.

A Special Guide, Number 11, has been inserted for *young people*. This is a new **first**, to my knowledge, and they are provided with maps to follow and learning games to play as they travel about the two states.

It is hoped you find pleasure from these **Travel Treats** as you *"poke"* about in Oregon and Northern California and add your own particular discoveries as you roam "God's Country".

WYNNE GIBSON, Author

ACKNOWLEDGEMENTS

It would be impossible to give adequate *"thanks"* to all the people who have helped me write this **Travel Treat** Guide. Everyone from innkeepers, restaurant managers, gas station attendants, to private individuals were most cooperative and added many pertinent items on their own. Their help and concern have really made this book possible.

A special tribute is made to my friend Charles Travers, the illustrator, whose skill and imagination bring lightness and humor to the traveler's journey and fun for the young people.

I am particularly grateful to my family and friends who have endured my peculiarities while writing this guide, who have read it, made valuable criticisms and comments, and aided me in every aspect. Ken and Virginia Bailey are singled out for their work in proofreading and editing each page, not only once, but twice. A special "bouquet" for grandaughter, Krista Foster, for her advice in the young people's section.

Last, acknowledgement is made to Panda and Dandy Langston who followed me into and out of every room in the house, visited many of the places firsthand, sat quietly with me from the incubation period to the final end of this new endeavor. This they did with great devotion and belief in my ability to persevere while they rested.

INDEX

BIG FOOT

NOTES:

Guide One

The United States is a land of many contrasts but nowhere are they more prevalent or more beautiful than in the great Northwest. Almost every American has a passing acquaintance with Captain Jack, the Modoc Indian; Fort Clatsop, OR., where Lewis and Clark ended their expedition from St. Louis; Crater Lake, the bluest in the world; and the Oregon Caves. But how many have heard of Crescent City's Tetrapods, the Lake that Wasn't There in New Pine Creek, CA., Mare's Eggs at Fort Klamath, OR., and the State of Jefferson?

As I drove homeward along the Redwood Highway, #199, amid the shadows of the lacy-leafed, long-branched, towering redwood trees, also known as Sequoia "big tree" after the half breed Cherokee Indian Sequoyah, I could not resist the temptation to stop for a brief moment in the enchanted forest. It was ten o'clock in the morning but the lanceolate branches of the 2000 year old giants still hid the rays of the early April sunshine. Birds and little forest creatures moved about the evergreen trees and tangled undergrowth enjoying their morning outing.

I had just completed a 1500 mile journey covering the northern coast of California from Eureka to Ship Ashore at Smith River, Highway 101. From there I went to Brookings, OR., and up the some 400 miles of rugged but spectacular scenic Oregon coast to Astoria, Oregon. Leaving Highway 101, I meandered down Highway 30 from Portland to Biggs following the Columbia Gorge. Highway 97 at Biggs took me through Redmond, Bend, Klamath Falls, then on to Lakeview, CA., and New Pine Creek, CA. From Lakeview to Redding, I followed Highway 395 through Willow Ranch, Davis Creek, Alturas, changed over to Highway 299 out of Canby and on into Redding, CA. on I-5. On I-5, I doubled back to Dorris, Weed, Mt. Shasta, Dunsmuir, and returned to Redding. Completing the loop, I wove my way back to Eureka via the majestic Trinity Alps, Highway 299, through one of the supposed homes of Big Foot. I had read and heard of the many jewels of history and heritage that lay waiting for the interested along this part of the West and I had not been disappointed.

Whether an armchair traveler, tourist, or historian, join me as I take a few minutes rest beside the fallen redwood tree, pour myself a cup of coffee, and listen to the sounds of the primeval forest. Let me become your guide and tour with me through the places, sights, sounds, and meet people I have just visited.

Del Norte County in northern California holds many tourist treasures. Eureka, one of the biggest cities dotting the northern coast, relies mainly on fishing, logging, lumber, and recreation. Old Town encompassing 1st, 2nd, 3rd or "C" to "G" streets, retains the original buildings reminiscent of raucous days of the early city. There is Old Town Art Guild on "F" Street and a boutique showing hand crafted items. Redwood Acres has stock car racing, art shows, horse shows and fairs along with other events scheduled throughout the year. Sequoia Park contains 52 acres of virgin redwoods where there is to be found a zoo, children's playground, formal gardens, trails, picnic facilities, softball fields. And, of course, what would the coast be without fishing . . . which is usually good to excellent. Many of the "ginger bread" homes, the wooden office buildings, old-time saloons in the reconstructed harbor area, are still in use. It is indeed, worth your time and photographs to stop awhile in Eureka.

Leaving Eureka, we pass through Trinidad, Orick, Klamath, Requa. At Requa we stop briefly to see the old Yuorok Indian family house called "Rekwai". Built of redwood slabs hewn with an elk horn, it is considered probably the oldest residence in California.

As we are in no hurry, and our aim is to learn the history of the past, we will detour a short distance and follow the historic stagecoach road connecting Crescent City to Grants Pass. Within a few miles on the Old Stage Road we stop and gaze in awe at the Stout Memorial tree (redwood) which stands 340 feet tall, God's handiwork.

A few miles more and we are in Crescent City. This small seaport town was almost wiped out in 1964 after being hit by a Tsunami tidal wave on Good Friday . . . the tidal wave an aftermath of the Alaskan earthquake. Twenty-one blocks were obliterated but it has been rebuilt into a clean, modern, thriving city boasting a good-sized shopping mall, convention center, and Olympic size municipal pool. Campgrounds and R.V. facilities abound.

As you enter the city limits, you notice a strange looking oddity called a "tetrapod", meaning "having four feet". This city was the first in the Western hemisphere to use the French invented tetrapods and over 1,975 of the 25 ton monsters are placed in the seaward side of the breakwater and interlaced to keep the heavy seas from destroying the harbor. They worked well and the city paid tribute by setting a tetrapod as a sentinel to their gates.

We're in luck. We have made it in time to visit the Battery Point lighthouse built in 1856. It stands 200 yards off-shore and can be visited only at low tide when visitors can walk across the ocean floor to browse through the old photographs and relics of famous old ships that sailed in and out of Crescent City harbor.

One of the tragedies was the oil tanker S. S. Emidio. It was torpedoed by the Japanese in WWII in nearby waters, drifted into Crescent City channels and sank. A plaque is displayed on "H" Street commemorating the heroic crew.

July 30, 1865, the coastwise steamer "Brother Jonathan" was wrecked off the St. George Reef at Crescent City. Of the 232 passengers and crew only 19 were saved. Many of the victims are buried in what is now known as "Brother Jonathan" cemetery.

We take a quick look at the famed Citizen's Dock where the fishing fleet unloads catches of dungeness crab, shrimp, and other ocean fish. Each February the World Championship Dungeness Crab races are held at the fairgrounds. The race is open to all "fellow-crabs" and the Crescent City Chamber of Commerce will pit their own "Cassius Crab", who is renowned for being the fightingest, meanest crab in the world, against them all. The crabs are put into individual stalls and prodded and coaxed by masters to gain the finish line first. The super attraction afterwards is the dungeness crab feed, at nominal prices, and all you can eat.

Speaking of eating, it is about time for lunch. About five miles out of Crescent City the highway forks, 101 to the left and 199 returns to the interior. We take 101 for another five miles to dine at Ship Ashore located at the mouth of the Smith River, overlooking the Pacific Ocean. Ship Ashore combines the romance of the sea, the majesty of the redwoods, the thrill of water sports, and comfort of fine accommodations. The Galley dining room features fine food at reasonable prices. It is a Best Western motel and has 32 units and can accommodate 300 travel trailers/mobile homes. The 160 foot former luxury yacht, which served with the US Navy during WWII, has been beached and the top deck serves as a souvenir and gift shop and the bottom deck is a museum and famous "Pirates Den".

5

It was a warm, languid April day and after a leisurely lunch, we decided to go back to the junction and take Highway 199 to Patrick's Creek Lodge, about a thirty minute drive.

Originally called Partridge Creek Lodge because of the abundance of partridges in the area, it was built by George Dunne high on the Gasque toll road in the Oregon Mountains. George Dunne was later murdered for his gold, it is said, and in 1910 the Lodge was sold to Eusede and Charlotte Raymond. When the mines closed in that area and the new road went in a few miles down the mountain, the Raymonds rebuilt the Lodge and called it Patrick's Creek Lodge after the creek nearby. Charlotte became known as "Lottie" and she never lacked for boarders or guests. She served excellent food and clean lodgings. The Raymond family weathered many financial reverses and two fires but stuck it out until Eusede died and Lottie was too old to carry on the business and it was sold in 1947.

However, according to past owners and many guests, Lottie has never left her home. They recount stories of her ghost rearranging silverware on tables, moving pans and other items about the kitchen, and prowling through the corridors at night. The Lodge stands intact and is now complemented by a small motel and swimming pool. The dining room is surrounded by glass windows and plants abound. The food remains excellent and the lodgings clean. During the nine months it is open, many guests return to the high mountains for fine cuisine, relaxation and cool beauty of the tree-covered mountains.

On the way back, we pass through Jedediah Smith Sta'e Park which is in the midst of towering redwoods. Here you will find outstanding facilities for picnicking, swimming, camping. A little history of the redwood tree . . . it was once found in many parts of the world but now grows only in a narrow strip along the northern California coast and parts of Oregon. Species date back more than 30 million years. The understory is thick with shrubs such as rosebay, rhododendron, salal, and huckleberry, small wild flowers and ferns. Here time seems to stand still and you can appreciate the natural forest living at a pace and rhythm all its own.

By the time we reach the junction and return to Highway 101, it is getting dusk. We pass hundreds of lily fields on our way north. These are grown for bulb sales and shipped overseas. Smith River community is known as the Easter Lily Capital of the World which they celebrate with pomp and circumstance each July.

As we drive along each new curve and bend in the road, the scenery is ever-changing until finally the huge red and orange sun falls abruptly into the blue of the white capped Pacific Ocean. We cross the line into Oregon, enter Harbor, cross the bridge into Brookings, and even though it is getting dusk, drive about 30 miles on to Gold Beach.

We could have stayed at one of the many quality motels at Brookings, as we will be doubling back to Harbor tomorrow, but Ireland's Rustic Lodge is one of the old and special places to stop overnight on the southern Oregon coast.

For many years Ireland's original owners would arrange to bring you a never to-be-forgotten, home-cooked dinner to your private Logette but while that is no longer possible, the present management boasts a new two-story motel plus eight Logettes with fireplaces. Rooms are clean and tastefully decorated and each has its own beach area. The grounds are often considered one of the city's private parks by travelers as they are so well tended. They are used for weddings and local special events . . . you need your camera.

We have dinner at one of the area's well known restaurants Jot's, where the sole and halibut entrees are relished. Jot's too provides well-appointed rooms, each with sliding glass doors overlooking the busy Rogue River with its fishermen, sightseers, and panoramic view of the surrounding waterway, mountains and city.

The "skip and a jump" drive back to Ireland's Rustic Lodge allowed us the pleasure of seeing the city's night lights, the moon, and the giant Pacific Ocean lolling peacefully upon the sandy shore. We reflected on the day's experiences and looked forward to tomorrow's surprises.

INDEX

NOTES:

Guide Two

We have many places to go and things to see. We rise early. A faint skift of fog foams about the city's edge but stays briefly. The sun has colored the city gold, to match its name,by the time of our departure. We travel slowly back to Brookings relishing the fresh morning scents, the change-of-guard scene as the moon left the horizon and the sun took charge through the lifting fog.

Brookings sits at the mouth of the Chetco River with timber, fishing, flower bulb raising the economic mainstays. It boasts an unusually mild climate and it is known for its azaleas. Each Memorial Day weekend, the well-publicized Azalea Fesitival is held in the 26-acre Azalea State Park of-fHighway 101. Acres of daffodils bloom in February and March, and in July the countryside is covered in blossoming, fragrant Easter lilies.

Before driving northward, we have been invited to visit Viola Hanscam, 91 years old and a resident of Harbor, south of Brookings across the Chetco Bridge. Viola is a woman of many firsts in her lifetime and she recently received another honor . . . Pioneer Citizen. One of her outstanding feats is her handmade rag rugs depicting her family's history. Seated in the living room of the home she and her husband built, a steaming cup of coffee in hand, this bright-eyed, enthusiastic woman proceeded to tell us of the famed rugs.

"The rugs were made from used clothes of the Hanscam family. They are 35" long and 13" wide to fit the stairs in this house. The first rug goes back to 1911 when I left home to get married. It shows me leaving my parents' home and traveling by foot and wagon to Grants Pass. Rug Two is of our homestead with bunkhouse, cookhouse and our two daughters. Rug Three adds our two sons, the store we opened in Kerby, our house and the schoolhouse. The Masonic Temple, Oddfellows Lodge, barbershop, and a new son are shown in Rug Four. Rug Five depicts the move to Fort Dick, California, in 1924. I put in redwood trees, the new store we opened, and our four sons. Rug Six follows our move to Harbor, Oregon . . . the new store there and the row of cabins behind with the Chetco River along the top. The last rug, Seven, was done in 1961. It replaces the old store with the new one and the cabins are gone. Lifestyles changed considerably from the time I started the rugs until they were finished."

"I understand these rugs were placed on display at the

11

University of Oregon, then to the Oregon Historical Society Museum in Portland, and on to the Renwick Gallery at the Smithsonian Institute in Washington, D.C.?" I queried.

"Yes," Viola said, "I was very proud to have them selected for such an honor. They were returned from Washington, D.C., and hung in the Oregon State House, Salem, until July 1981, with the Webfoot, BunchGrassers Oregon Folk Art Gallery. They are now on display at the Harbor local Museum."

Viola still finds time to keep current the family's photo album collection, raise a large vegetable and flower garden, babysit greatgrandchildren and serves on the board of directors for the Curry County Historical Society. She has an "Open Door" to all who are interested in her lifetime of living projects and Southern Oregon Coast history. The early morning coffee and thirty minutes spent with Viola Hanscam started the day just right.

We pass through rugged headlands and bluffs rising straight from the seas as we drive back from Brookings to Gold Beach. This is the home of some of the most rugged and wild of Oregon's coastal scenery. The road dips and climbs and curves and climbs again. We pass Whale's Head Cove, a State Park and a noted picnic and beach area. Oregon State Parks are some of the finest. We glimpse a small group of sea lions frolicking in their habitat, and enjoy the salty fragrance of the ocean, the cool breeze, and surf-washed coastline. We will take the time to explore Gold Beach before driving on.

For bridge watchers, there are 17 grand and graceful, concrete arched bridges along the Oregon coast. Rogue River bridge at Gold Beach is one of the more elaborate with sunburst designs on the entrance pylons and seven graceful arches spanning the three-eighth mile structure. The main part of Gold Beach sits on the south side of the bridge with the tiny hamlet of Wedderburn on the north. Fishermen cast their lines here the year around . . . Chinook and silver salmon, steelhead, and up the river, trout. Agate lovers, beachcombers, and clammers are all over. It is famous for its jet-boat trips to Agness, 32 miles up the Rogue River, or you can go on to Paradise Gorge, 52 miles, which is the wild river part of the canyon. Daily trips are made, May through October, by US mail boats or Jerry's Jets. Both depart in the morning and return mid-afternoon. Lunch can be arranged at Agness with home style coooking or you can pack your own picnic basket. Passengers making the trip will enjoy the wild, scenic beauty of the forest, see deer, bear, raccoon, bald eagles, blue heron, and patches of colorful wildflowers as the boat pilot tells you the tales of the old river.

As we move through Gold Beach, we stop at Jot's Resort on the north side, walk around the dock area, check the fishermen's lunch, and have a bit of breakfast.

Midway between historic Port Orford and Gold Beach is the Prehistoric Rain Garden . . . one of the most unusual attractions in the world. This is the Rain Forest that recreated a world of lifesize replicas of dinosaurs and other prehistoric animals among profusely growing, primitive plants. You will be transported back through time as you stroll among the luxuriant ferns and moss covered trees and follow the weird forms of animal life that disappeared from this earth over 70 million years ago. It is a children's paradise.

Rain forests are located in small coastal valley pockets, surrounded by hills, and protected from fierce winter storms. The climate must be mild, few winds, rich soil, and exceptionally heavy rainfall (6 to 10 feet a year). This brings about the supergrowing, giant, lush undercover . . . skunk cabbages with elephant ear tropical leaves, trees that live for hundreds of years, and innumerable mosses and ferns cascading from the trees. Rain forests range from Northern California to British Columbia but few are accessible on the main highway as is this one. Our unhurried tour of twenty minutes brings us from the deep caverns of the dense forest to the sparkling morning sunshine of here and now. We pick up a souvenir and travel north.

Port Orford, a semi-retirement town, sits gracefully on the irregular, craggy mountainside jutting into the sapphire Pacific. Many of its inhabitants swear by its curing effects on their health problems.

Bandon moves into view. In 1936, it was practically wiped out by fire and acres of forest and wildlife were destroyed. An abandoned lighthouse at the south end of the Coquille River was one of the few structures left standing after the fire. Each September this friendly little town hosts a cranberry festival and if you would like to visit a cranberry bog, this is your opportunity. The weather is usually delightful in September, and the berries are harvested in October and November.

Moving on to Coos Bay and North Bend, we will stop for lunch at the Thunderbird Inn one of the many fine A-rated restaurants and accommodations in the twin cities. They are connected by the mile long McCullough steel bridge with deco-style spires at the entrance. This is one of Oregon's larger harbor shipping facilities. It is a busy waterway for foreign and domestic shipping but it is also a fisherman and small boater's delight. Clammers and crabbers walk the beaches. Scheduled scenic tours of the bay leave from the waterfront for a cruise of the waters surrounding the largest towns on the south coast. Here you will want to take time to visit the many myrtlewood shops for decorative articles made by craftsmen at local factories and shops. This is myrtlewood country. For picnickers, visit North Bend's Simpson Park, a greenery tipped oasis. You will also find the museum where you can browse through Indian and pioneer exhibits. The canopied and cobblestoned Coos Bay Mall is vibrant with trees and flowerbeds in summer and you may find a flower show, art or other craft exhibit outside, if weather permits.

When nature passed out scenery, Oregon came in with almost a full hand. North of Coos Bay we come to the Oregon Dunes, now a national recreation area. A short ride on a dune buggy is a must. We will hire a buggy from one of the private operators and let them do the driving as one must be careful for shallow pockets of quicksand behind the foredune where the buggy can quickly become mired. We bounce along with the wind in our hair and specks of sand floating around us. Seagulls and other shore birds around Bluebill Lake fill the air. It is a never-to-be forgotten experience. The Dunes can also be viewed from a little train that traverses the sand mounds . . . backpackers, fishermen, clammers, beachcombers are everywhere. The sand shifts daily and moves about two feet a year. Clear blue lakes appear and disappear between the valleys of the ever-moving, yellow-colored grains of dust.

There are so many places of intrigue and interest to stop, but many will have to be left for the next trip. Now on to Florence near the home of the Sea Lion Caves. Sea lion bulls from the Bering Sea return yearly to their ancestral home in the spring to mate. The sea lions cluster around Sea Lion Point where they live the year around mating and rearing their young pups. When you descend to the caves, you hear hundreds of them barking, causing an unbelievable din. The bull sea lions have harems of from ten to twenty cows. The cubs are usually born in June. During stormy weather, they stay inside the caves but good weather finds them assembled on the long rock ridge or playing in the waves. These caves

14

house the largest sea grotto in North America and one of the few privately owned scenic wonders on the Oregon coast. The caves also contain the rarely seen pigeon guillemot. To reach the caves, you can either walk the steps or take the elevator. As it is about 1500 feet down; most opt to take the elevator.

As a little aside, when we passed through the town of Gardner, we noticed a grocery store marquee with the friendly message "COME IN. LETTUCE MEAT EWE."

We drive on to Heceta (Huh-SEE-ta), a beautiful headland jutting far out into the crashing waves and visit the lighthouse named for Bruno Heceta, Spanish Sea Captain.

A short stop is made at Darlingtonia Botanical Wayside 18-acre estate. It has been designated a protected area for the cobra lily or pitcher plant and a wooden walkway allows you to get a "bird's eye view" of the insect eating plants.

Yachats (YAH-hots) is known for its fishing and Silver Smelt Fry in July. Had we been going to stay overnight, we would have picked the Yachats Lodgettes or Shamrock Inn as they were indeed attractive but our destination was Salishan between Newport and Lincoln City.

Newport. Seasons make little difference to the naturalists who flock here the year around. Here you will find Oregon's largest tidepool area, marine fossils, recorded ancient sea life, and migratory geological activity. Winter is a special time for wildlife with clouds of wintering birds sailing about, rain or shine, and whales frolicking on their southward migration. From the mudflats of Yaquina Bay to the South Jetty it is a laboratory of nature. Idaho Flats boasts one of Oregon's largest collections of shorebirds, ducks, and gulls. If you visit after high-tide, birds are concentrated in the first strip of food rich tideflats. The South Jetty is a fine spot for beachcombing but visitors should be aware of high waves, high tides, and drifting logs.

Newport has a wax museum on Highway 101 displaying over 50 lifesize figures of historical importance. Minutes away from the Wax Museum is a lively collection of life beneath the sea. These sea animals and plants inhabit 500,000 gallons of filtered sea water at the Under Sea Gardens and can be seen by visitors through viewing windows. Daily shows fascinate audiences and particularly the children as the divers move through the waters to tickle the sea urchins, tease the wolf eels, and hug the octopi. It is also of interest to note that the Oregon State University

15

Marine Science Center is headquartered at Newport.

Time is getting short and we move on to Yaquina Bay and drive a short distance to the Yaquina Bay lighthouse built in 1871. It was used only three years and then a more efficient beacon was built three miles north. However, it is interesting to view the recently refurnished lighthouse and see the typical items used. All along this shoreline you will see surfers riding the waves, sailors bravely battling the windy waters, fishermen throwing in or taking out their lines, boats heading out for deep sea fishing, and clammers and crabbers carrying the tools of their trade. There is a four hour sightseeing tour of the area and when you finish, if you are a crab lover, you can buy one right out of a steaming pot or stop at one of the good restaurants along the waterfront.

It is now late afternoon and the sunny day has changed the green and blue of the Pacific waters into silver with a slight cast of gold sprayed upon the waves. We will be staying overnight at Salishan Lodge but another very fine accommodation is The Inn at Spanish Head perched on the side of a cliff with a magnificent view of the ocean and beach access.

The sun falls dramatically into the ocean as we drive into Gleneden Beach, Oregon, Salishan Lodge. Footsteps of foraging Indians a thousand years ago, footsteps of homesteaders a hundred years ago, footsteps of animals, past and present, and now our own as we become part of the family of guests at the Lodge.

It is built of local stone, massive beams, various regional woods to convey the beauty and strength of Oregon and the Northwest. Works of Northwest artists have been used throughout the Lodge to add further dimensions to the image of native scenery. In addition to the public works of artists, there are over 300 original prints, drawings and watercolors in individual guest rooms. It is elegance in the serenity of a forest setting and has been named a consistent winner of the Mobil Travel Guide 5-Star rating as one of the best guest accommodations in the country. There are 150 guest rooms, each with fireplace, view balcony, oversize beds, and covered parking at the door. Swimming pool, golf course, hiking, beach access, children's playground, trails, tennis, and special activities are all included.

This evening, although tired, we were hungry, and reservations were made in the Gourmet Room and the "Breast of Chicken" was supreme. As we dally over our glass of wine, we hear a fellow traveler ask, "What does a vacationer do here?" People don't come to the Oregon cost to DO anything. They come to relax, watch the ocean, fish, beachcomb, hike, crab, clam, observe, read, golf, swim, learn, and meet the native Oregonians who are a friendly pioneer people.

A slight mist of fog wafts past our window as we open the blind to watch the full moon cast its luminous rays on the restless waves of the vast western ocean. It has been another glorious day.

INDEX

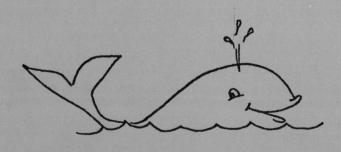

NOTES:

Guide Three

We slept a little late, our third day of travel, so we settled for a quick cup of coffee, a buttered roll and started on our way. The morning was somewhat cool but we set our car thermostat a bit higher and thought of the pioneers who had traveled this last outpost of the western frontier without such comforts.

Neskown, Nahalem, Neahkahnie, Necanicum, Clatskanie were a few of the Indian named hamlets passed. Even though the hour was early, the docks were busy with fishermen, and the shores teeming with people ocean watching and savoring the early morning hour.

Lincoln City, a booming tourist city in the summer when its population of 5000 often doubles or triples, is a short distance from Salishan. It is the center of the 20 Miracle Miles of oceanside resorts, motels, galleries, shops and tourist attractions. Deep-sea fishing is plentiful as is coastal catch and lakes and rivers offer their "catch of the day" for those who favor inland fishing. Elegant accommodations line the beaches, cliffs, and bluffs. Less expensive, fully equipped cottages are also available as are campsites and picnic areas. Here, you will find locals and tourists fishing on their lunch hour at Devil's Lake. The children are captivated at Lacey's Dollhouse and delighted at Pixieland's fun, games and rides. These two attractions are open daily from June through Labor Day.

A few miles later we come into Tillamook which was reduced to ashes in 1933 when 400 square miles of prime timberland was destroyed. In 1939 and 1945, forest fires again took their toll. Oregonians put their money and minds to work and, through reforestation, today young trees are again growing to adulthood in the Tillamook Burn.

Cannon Beach, so-named for the cannon that washed ashore in 1846, is between Tillamook Head and Arch Cape. Rising 235 feet above the sea is the giant Haystack Rock which houses both marine and bird life. Time out was taken to watch the myriad shapes and sizes of sealife move about in the tidepools at the base of the immense rock.

Arch Cape, nearby, is supposed to have buried treasure left by a mystery ship hidden on Neahkahnie Mountain. So far, no one has found it, but who knows, you might be just the lucky one.

Seaside and we *must* drive the famed promenade and see

the outstanding old beach houses still home to some of the younger generations of original pioneer families who built there. Seaside is a major convention center with fine accommodations. There is an excellent aquarium exhibit. The Necanicum River, rarely without its share of salmon, steelhead and trout, cuts through the center of town and is one of the City's focal points. There is always something going on . . . marathons in August and February, Miss Oregon pageant in July, Beachcombers Festival in February and arts and crafts shows in March and August.

Astoria, in Clatsop County, sits almost on the tip of the northwest corner of Oregon. It is ten miles from the Pacific Ocean, on the mouth of the Columbia River. Astoria is a special place and has a special history. It is named after John Jacob Astor of New York who started the Pacific Fur Company on the Columbia River. Fort Astoria was the first permanent American settlement on the Pacific Coast. The Fort passed into British hands during the War of 1812 and was returned to the United States in 1818. The county was named Clatsop for the Clatsop Indians . . . a branch of the Oregon Chinook tribe. The Columbia River was so called after Captain Robert Gray's ship *The Columbia* . . . the first to enter the harbor. Astoria's population is now about 10,000. Nearby Fort Clatsop was the headquarters of Lewis and Clark expedition in 1805-06 and it has been rebuilt into an exact replica of the original Fort and named a national monument.

The early morning cup of coffee and roll have long disappeared, and our appetite can no longer be ignored. Before pursuing our sightseeing tour of this historic town, we will brunch at the Thunderbird Motor Inn. The Seafare Restaurant is a particularly restful spot for stimulating the gastric juices. The Inn is built over the water and the view has all the charm for which the city is famous. You can hear the gently lapping water, the cry of the seagull and the churning of fishing boats as they head out to sea. Our refreshing crab/shrimp salad and glass of Reisling white wine renewed our zest and anticipation of the travel treats in store for us the rest of the day.

About 1900, Astoria was as big and splashy as San Francisco and wealthy merchants and sea captains vied in building prestigious homes on the hillsides. Fire in 1922 destroyed the majority of them but of the dozen or so that remained, most have been restored to their former glory.

Flavel House, between Duane and Exchange streets, contains many artifacts of the area. Astoria harbor . . . first shipping center in the West . . . is still a busy, bustling sea port . . . ships from all over the world, enter their harbor. Seconds turn into minutes, as you watch the varied activities taking place throughout the waterfront. A *must see* is the Astoria Column. Built in 1926, the column measures 125 feet from top to bottom and stands on the peak of the 635 foot Coxcomb Hill and a well-tended park surrounds the base. The murals, or graffiti, on the column show scenes of Northwest history occurring around the Astoria area. It was designed by E. D. Kirtchfield, New York, who patterned the triumphal arch of the column after those in Emperor Trojan's time. On a clear day, the view of the river and nearby coastlands is indescribable. It is one of those experiences one has to do firsthand to savor the full effect. Astoria, after 11 years of working toward its goal, now has one of the best maritime collection museums. There is an admission charge.

Every one of the hundred and thirty minutes used exploring Astoria has been our gain. We now take Highway 30 towards Portland, Oregon's largest city, where we follow the Columbia River as it twists and turns and the car noses its way through quiet, wooded countryside and gently sloping farmlands. At Westport, a toll ferry carries cars around the wooded Puget Island and over to Cathlamet, WA. As we proceed through the old river towns of Rainier, Columbia City, St. Helens, we return to the slow-paced era of the 1800's.

From the time we left the great Sunset Empire of the Oregon Coast this morning until we reach the outskirts of Portland, we have passed through a vacationer's wonderland. Picnicking, boating, camping, fishing, clamming, hunting, golfing, surfing, hiking, swimming, sightseeing and historical sites by the hundreds, places of amusement for the children . . . one can ask, *What is there to do in Oregon?*

Portland, the City of Roses, is also proud of its flowering rhododendrons, azaleas, forsythia, Scotch broom, and wildflowers which bloom in profusion as spring and summer emerge. With a population of over a million people, it is a thriving small metropolis. As you walk down Broadway, one of the main downtown streets, you find trees and landscaping on almost every corner. Neighborhood parks are many and because of the closeness of the Japanese current, it has a very

23

mild, somewhat wet, climate. Modern transportation . . . boats, busses, trains . . . will arrange sightseeing tours through the labyrinth of parks, gardens, scenic drives, Old Town, the waterfront, historic areas, modern buildings, the Columbia River, the Columbia Gorge, you name it. We will return in Guide Eight to cover the pleasures of Portland and surrounding communities. A good three days will be required to see the more important places, drive about and get a feel for "the biggest small town in the West".* (*Sunset, Oregon . . . 1980) We will then follow I-5 down to Ashland in southwest Oregon and what a trip that is.

The Columbia River is some 80 miles in length. We are going to follow it to Biggs where we will turn off and take Highway 97 through central Oregon. At Troutdale, we leave IS-84 and drive the Columbia Scenic Highway. It is a two lane, good-condition highway. Instead of running parallel to the river it climbs upward through acres of ferns, forests, and flowers with parks every few miles and arrives at Crown Point some 700 feet above the river. Endless waterfalls cascade over cliffs, bluffs ending in the breathtaking Multnomah Falls . . . falling some 600 feet down. To try and drive and look and keep within the speed limit, is no easy task. If time allows the traveler, foot trails are everywhere for investigaion. Take the time, however, to stop at Bonneville Dam, built in 1937, and view the salmon and steelhead coming up the fish ladder. It will certainly aid the children's education and maybe your own. While you watch the ship's locks operate, the children can make use of the children's playground. Just beyond the Bridge of the Gods, you come to the Cascade Locks, the first on the Columbia. The houses, built a hundred years ago, continue to serve as the lock master's home.

Columbia Gorge Hotel on the Hood River has been restored and serves fine food. Built in the 1920's, the old and the new have been combined to please both the palate and the artistic tastes of the guests. For those preferring the modern . . . there is the Hood River Inn, a clean, well-rated motel.

The Dalles, in Wasco county, is the end of the Oregon Trail. Figures etched on the rocks nearby show that thousands of years ago, before white man ever invaded the wilderness, someone from the far north had lived there. Indians, centuries later, met in the same spot to swap meat, fish, and grain. Today, it continues as a trading area for the central Oregon farms and orchards. Wasco County originally in-

24

cluded some 130,000 square miles . . . from the Cascades to the Rockies and from the Columbia River to the California border.* (*Sunset, Oregon, 1980) It was the largest county ever formed in the United States and ultimately, 17 other counties were formed from this one. The City of the Dalles has many historic sites such as the old courthouse, 1850. It has been made into the city's museum. St. Paul's Church, 1875, St. Peter's Catholic Church, 1897. There is also a special museum of exhibits on Bigfoot or Sasquatch reported as seen in many areas of the Northwest. He is supposedly an off-shoot of the Abominable Snowman of the Himalayas. For those wanting to tour the Dalles Dam, a red, white and blue train leaves every half hour between 10 a.m. and 6 p.m.

We now leave the lush, prolific, dense forests, ferns, and fauna and take our last view of the majestic Columbia River. At Biggs, Highway 97, the scenery changes abruptly, and the sun, sans trees, turns the beginning of the high plateau into semi-arid county. It has a beauty all its own, but the change is somewhat drastic.

A brief note for those with a few extra hours or day or two, cross the bridge at Biggs to the Washington side and visit the Maryhill Museum of Fine Arts which houses one of the best art collections of the Pacific Northwest. While on that side of the river, drive a few more miles and see the American town of Stonehenge. Sam Hill, a railroad tycoon, wanted to commemorate those who died in WWI, but the project never seemed to get off the ground and it has become somewhat of a ghost town.

At this point, we have covered over 250 miles and the shadows of late afternoon are following us. By the time we reach Redmond, we will have observed about all the mind and body can take for one day.

Redmond Inn is our accommodation for the night and it is right on the highway which is convenient. The Reservation Clerk finds our reservation quickly, is friendly and helpful. This graciousness was impressive when we were tired and anxious to get to our room. The Inn does not have a restaurant but they recommended several and there is one next door.

After making ourselves presentable, we chose Mrs. Beasley's family style dining and within walking distance. They also serve cocktails. We were hungry, as usual, and there was little left of the steak, baked potato and homemade hot biscuits but we managed to top it off with a piece of

25

homemade chocolate cake and ice cream.

We concluded that tomorrow we must slow our pace a little. This was Big Country and we would have to do quite a lot of driving to visit the places we had on our list. We would explore the nearby areas, talk to some of the local people, and make Klamath Falls, about 170 miles, our evening's destination.

As we turned out the lights and opened the drapes, our moon was still with us. Was that the howl of a coyote? No, it couldn't be . . . we were tired and it must be our imagination, but, could it be?

INDEX

NOTES:

Guide Four

We knew there would be few restaurants on today's drive, and we ate a hearty breakfast. The morning was what the high plateau people would call "nippy". The dew, glazed with a slight touch of ice, shimmered on the car windows and we felt quite comfortable in our sweaters. We remembered good walking shoes.

We planned to start for Prineville, some 19 miles east, return to Madras, Highway 97, and proceed to the once ghost-towns of Shaniko and Antelope, return for lunch at Kan-Nee-Ta on the Warm Springs Indian Reservation. We would then see what developed for the afternoon depending on the time left.

Redmond, named for homesteader Frank I. Redmond in 1906, has a population of approximately 6500 with an over-all trading area of 15,000. However, by the year 2000, it is bracing for an influx of some 10,000 additional people attracted by the electronic industries planning or in the process of building in nearby sites. Moving from a strictly agricultural-lumbering economy will take some adjusting but the people in this community have always learned how to adjust.

The railroad came to Redmond in 1917, and it became a thriving trade center. Temperatures are rarely above 90 degrees in the summer and 40-50 at night. Below freezing temperatures are the norm in the winter with snowfall around 15-17 inches. These temperatures make for an invigorating climate all year around and sports abound. Here, the natural beauty brings forth campers, rockhunters, river floaters, campers, fishermen, hikers, skiers, snowmobilers, photographers, and the list goes on.

In Prineville, we take a short time to browse through Crook County's pioneer courthouse, Juniper Art gallery, tour the historical houses and note that the small town has 23 churches. We pass several city parks, swimming pool, tennis courts, bike and jogging paths. Prineville, the oldest city in Central Oregon, is on the coast-to-coast bicentennial bicycle route.

Pinnacles, canyons, plateaus . . . Smith Rock State Park offers rock climbing challenges for both the beginner and the expert. We stopped the car to view the 403 foot deep gorge carved by the Crooked River as it twists and turns through the countryside. The beautiful Metolious River, beginning from mountain springs, wanders dramatically over the countryside and you marvel at the wonders created by stone and water. Hundreds of campsites surround the Prineville and Ochoco reservoirs. Reindeer Ranch and Peterson Rock Gardens provide recreation, entertainment for the entire family. Mr. Peterson started gathering native volcanic rocks and gems as a hobby years ago. Over the years he has made them into exhibits of castles, statues, pools, miniature forts and, to top it off the White House with an American flag in front.

We are now a few miles from Shaniko on Highway 97. The tiny, almost forgotten town had an approximate population of 54 until several years ago when the Rajneesh group with their following of hundreds, settled in the area. Before that, the town centered around the Shaniko Hotel owned by Sue Morelli. The modern post office building and Standard gasoline station seem out of place as you view the original fire hall, general store, saloon and the Shaniko Hotel in this semi-deserted ghost-town.

In reminiscing with Sue Morelli, I learned that she came with her husband some 25 years ago from Portland. Here, he farmed a large section of land and ran cattle. They bought the old hotel containing 28 rooms and kept it open seven days a week-24 hours a day. Ten rooms were available for tourists and Sue served home-cooked food. The facilities were old but clean. However, progress eventually brought doom. Sue could not afford to invest the money to bring the old hotel up to required safety, fire and sanitation standards and it was closed. There were many attempts to re-open the hotel and reconstruct the historical city but they failed. Finally, the many valuable antique items in the hotel were auctioned off. Ed Ritter paid $4,800 for the 95 year old bar and $1000 apiece for the chandeliers.

In the early '80's considerable controversy erupted when the Bhagwan Shree Rajneesh moved his headquarters on a 64,000 acre ranch between Antelope and Shaniko. Guru Rajneesh has over 250,000 followers and about 500 spiritual centers throughout the world. The one near Antelope and Shaniko is one of the largest with 350 Rajneesh hands working its lands under the Guru's supervison. The town's appearance has certainly changed from the once wool center of the West to a spiritual mecca of western United States.

Antelope, even smaller than Shaniko, had twelve houses and about 40 residents prior to 1981. There was a store, post office and Bargain Center. The owners of the Bargain Store recalled that in 1976, Oregon's Senator Mark O. Hatfield presented the town with a U.S. flag honoring its 100 year anniversary. They said there were enough tourists and local customers to keep them busy and one could never outguess a customer. They recalled a day a man came in looking for a telephone booth to put in his home to keep his conversations private. Each of the twelve homes in Antelope had the name of its occupant hanging on the outside of the door . . . an old neighborly custom.

About 1981, followers of the Bhagwan Shree Rajneesh, Indian Guru, took over the area and town of Antelope and proceeded to incorporate it as their own city of Rajneeshpuram. Since their group arrived they have acquired a 100 square mile ranch commune 17 miles from Antelope with some 70 or more followers moving into Antelope, itself.

As we drove into and out of the two tiny towns of Shaniko and Antelope, we pondered their future . . . these two Western settlements settled by sheep men. Would they continue to be the pride of the people who settled this western area or was it to be a new beginning for an Indian Guru whose plans call for the city to grow to 3,800 by 1987?

We took the 11 mile trip from Madras to Warm Springs and then on to Kan-Nee-Ta on the Warm Springs Indian Reservation. By this time we were assailed by hunger and tired from walking and driving. Kan-Nee-Ta is owned and operated by the Confederated Indian Tribes of Warm Springs in the center of a half million acre Indian Reservation complete with working ranch and wild horses. It is an inviting and beautiful spot, where it is said, the sun shines over 300 days a year. You can rent a tepee for a weekend or a deluxe apartment with a private balcony and spectacular view. Go for a long walk, but be sure to check with Kan-Nee-Ta people before taking off into surrounding hills. Plan to enjoy the area at about two miles per hour. Kan-Nee-Ta Resort can boast that "Kit Carson bathed here" and you, too, will enjoy its wonderland. We dined on game hen baked in clay with Indian fry bread and blackberry jam in the Juniper room. It was delicious.

We had made the circle from Redmond, Prineville, Madras, Shaniko, Antelope and returned to Redmond. The Sisters was our next stop as we drove west on Hwy 126. The Sisters is named after the three majestic mountains that rise above forest covered country. These mountains were originally called Faith, Hope and Charity. We took a free wagon ride around the town, participated in a crafts festival, and bought several pieces of the local costume jewelry.

This small town did not get electricity until 1930 and it was not until 1951 that the streets were paved, but the good will and friendliness of the residents and business people gave evidence of the time honored, old-fashioned hospitality and service of the West. The Sisters dog sled races are held the first part of January, the Gem Rock show the Fourth of July weekend. The oldest craft in America, quilt-making, is displayed the first Saturday after the Fourth of July. Rodeo weekend draws over 600 runners from all over the Northwest to compete in a 6.2 mile course run. The second weekend in June the Biggest Little Show in the World is held offering some of the nation's top rodeo cowboys and the roughest, toughest rodeo stock in the Northwest competing. This also includes the wild horse race. Visiting The Sisters is indeed worth the 20 mile trip off the main highway.

Bend, a short distance from The Sisters and back on Hwy 97, is a magical name for outdoor enthusiasts of all ages. Spring and summer the Deschutes and Little Deschutes Rivers are fishermen's heaven. You can also ski in the morning and a few minutes later take your choice of golf, tennis, sunbathing, canoeing, or wandering into the desert to study the flora and fauna. Guided raft trips are available on the Deschutes and other rivers, stables provide horses for roaming the many riding trails; you can bicycle; you can rent or bring your own canoe, sailboat, windsurfer or outboard. There are many locations for snowmobiling in the wintertime and skiing at Mt. Bachelor has earned a worldwide reputation for its Alpine facilities and marvelous snow conditions with lifts and day lodges serving dozens of groomed runs. The new Nordic Center, some 22 miles west of Bend, has some 15 miles of groomed, interconnecting loop trails suited to beginners, families and experts in the art of skiing. Motor Inns and motels run the price gamut and there are innumerable local, state, and federal and private facilities for camping and R.V.'s.

We visited Lava Butte and Lava Lands where a paved road takes you to the top. Here you see massive black lava emitted from the ancient volcano. Small parts of the lava have blocked some places in the Deschutes River flow but they eventually form new channels.

At the Lava River Caves we rented a lantern and descended

the stairs to the interior. The tube runs from 35 to 50 feet in width and height of 58 feet. It gives you first hand insight into old volcanic activity. We did not take time to go through Lava Cast Forest. Back some 6000 years ago, hot lava poured around a living pine forest freezing the trees into "stone trees" or making casts around upright trees. Other trees were encased in horizontal positions. Eventually the trees rotted away leaving the forest of hollow lava tubes. For those choosing to spend a little more time in the Bend area, the Lava Cast Forest, which is the largest of its kind, should be included in their itinerary.

The Forest Service maintains a nursery on 70 acres of ground propagating young ponderosa and lodgepole pine trees that will be placed in national forests in eastern Oregon and Washington. The nursery is four miles out on Butler Market Road. They also have a laboratory on West 12th and Trenton Avenue where field studies are carried out on ecological factors and timber growth. Visitors are welcome.

Almost everyone has heard of Sunriver Resort fifteen miles southwest of Bend. Here visitors use bicycles and carts more than automobiles. Life here is oriented for outdoor living of all kinds. It has its own nature center and a resident naturalist conducts programs and field trips. Guest artists and crafts people conduct summer classes. In the winter snowshoe and ski touring enthusiasts tour the countryside at Mt. Bachelor.

The high side of Oregon is a vast panorama of plateaus, volcanic attractions, lava forests, lava caves, rockhounding, quality resorts, lake-side cabins, fine motels and trailer parks and R.V. sites. Many fine restaurants offer outstanding cuisine and the view of the snow-capped Cascade peaks, and cinder cones east of Bend are a few of the spectacular mountains to be seen in every direction. There are over 220 lakes and 235 miles of fishing streams. This country is known as "The Land of the 1000 Sunsets".

We take Highway 97 out of Bend and travel through many small towns until coming to Chemult where we begin looking for Hwy 138 which will take us into Crater Lake National Park.

Mt. Mazama, out of which came Crater Lake, was once a 12,000 foot mountain in the Cascade Range. When the tremendous explosion created the crater, lava in the form of a frothy super-heated pumice was blown out in huge quantities. Smaller eruptions continued spewing out lava in a series of avalanches, causing cracks to open beneath the volcano and several miles of molten rock drained away. These ejections and drainings left a vast cavity beneath the cone which could not support its own weight and collapsed into the void and Mt. Mazama was destroyed 6,600 years ago. Over the centuries the great hole has accumulated water from rain and snow and because day-to-day evaporation and seepage are balanced with precipitation, the water level remains quite constant. The lake was discovered June 1853 and was called Deep Blue Lake until 1869 when visitors from Jacksonville renamed it Crater Lake. Only six lakes in the world are deeper and the depth is measured at 1,932 feet.

Footing can be treacherous on this volcanic rock and soil so stay on the trails and observe all signs. Descent to the Lake is permitted on Cleetwood Trail and in the winter all are advised to stay off snow cornices on the caldera rim. Beware of bears and do not leave food in open containers. There are breath-taking views from almost every spot as you drive or walk around once proud Mt. Mazama, now Crater Lake, considered one of the many Wonders of the World. Dining facilities and lounge are open from mid-June to mid-September as well as a cafeteria that serves meals daily. In winter, on weekends and holidays, it is operated as a coffee shop serving light refreshments. Gasoline is not sold in the winter time and there are no storage, towing or repairing facilities available within the park.

Leaving Crater Lake we wend our way to Fort Klamath where we stop at Mare's Egg Spring. It is located about one half mile south of Forest Road 3334 on County Road 4. Actually, it is only a wide spot in the road and one must be careful or it can be missed. The mineral content and the temperature of the water are such that these "mare's eggs" are formed, and grow in all sizes. Some visitors have taken them home from their natural habitat only to find the egg eventually disintegrates when placed in other water. But, it is worth the drive to see another of nature's rare occurrences . . . a mare's egg.

The sun has set as we return on Hwy 62 to Klamath Falls. We try to compare this day of Oregon desert, high plateaus, volcanic activity, cinder cones such as Goose Nest, Goose Egg, Ethel, Ruth and Maud mountains with yesterday's forest, rivers, flowers, and ephemeral shimmering, dew covered evergreens. There is no comparison. They both stand on their own merit and their own individual beauty and

34

contrasts. It does take a little time for the mind to grasp how so much can be so different in such a few comparatively short miles.

As usual, we are glad to find our reservations at the Thunderbird Motel, on South Sixth Street awaiting. For dinner, we choose the Catch of the Day . . . Oregon Trout . . . with a bottle of one of Oregon's finest Reisling's and once again, come to the end of another wonderful day. Klamath Falls . . . what a pretty name, but no Falls.

INDEX

NOTES:

Guide Five

"Rock formations that confound geologists. Rivers that run backwards. Plants that grow where they don't belong. Reports of huge humanoids. The Klamath Mountains of northeastern California fanning southwestern Oregon are a jumble of rugged peaks carved by sinuous rivers and an evolutionary mystery that has long puzzled and fascinated scientists". Reprinted from *Klamath Knott* by David Rains Wallace by the Sierra Book Club. Reprinted by permission of Sierra Club Books. I could hardly put the book down and was still delving into the mysteries contained within its pages as I finished breakfast.

Not knowing where we would be when the sun pointed to the middle of the day, we had asked the restaurant to pack us a lunch. The sky was somewhat overcast and again, we dressed warmly and had on our walking shoes.

The Klamath Falls Chamber of Commerce has five Loop Tours but we had seen many of the scenic wonders yesterday coming from the north. We decided to drive around the southwest end of Klamath Lake and then proceed on to the Lava Beds. Klamath Lake is considered one of the largest lakes in the west. The mountain land surrounding it has changed little since the days when moccasined warriors followed forest trails. Magnificent great white pelicans surveyed us at a distance wondering whether we would be feeding them or if we were just taking pictures. We did both. We passed two handsome young buck mule deer on their way for morning water, and pheasants, quail and other morning birds moved about in great array, little concerned about us. The Klamath area is renowned for hunting and fishing and when the seasons are open, people of all ages are found in over twenty campgrounds near lakes, rivers, and reservoirs with guns, bows and arrows, and fishing poles trying their luck.

Klamath County and neighboring Jackson County are dotted with beautiful campgrounds and parks. To the north is Hagelstein Park, a beautiful spot for letting the children run. Collier State Park is about 20 miles farther north and houses the Collier State Park Logging Museum showing items used in logging operations many years ago. Next to it is Williamson Campground. On Hwy 62 is Fort Klamath Denton Resort for swimming, picnicking, fishing, and camping in a secluded wooded area. Huckleberry Mountain and Farewell Bend are camper's delights. Diamond Lake offers fishing, hunting, boating, and swimming with room for R.V.'s and campers. Union Creek Trail and campground are good for walking and puttering about. West on Hwy 66 is Topsy Campground, Tubb Springs, Hyatt Lake, Howard Prairie, and Emigrant Lake. Hwy. 140 brings you to Tomahawk ski area, Lake of the Woods, Four Mile Lake, Pacific Crest Trail, Willow Lake and Fish Lake. All good roads.

Klamath Falls is the county seat of Klamath County and the southern boundary is the California state line. The tribe of Indians who inhabited this part of the country was the "Clamitt". Levi Scott, Applegate, Fremont and Kit Carson all passed this way and in 1863 Fort Klamath was established about 37 miles north of Klamath Falls. Linkville was founded in 1867 and the name changed to Klamath Falls in 1906. The metropolitan area now has a population of about 50,000. It has a high, dry climate with warm summers and usually mild winters. Logging, cattle, and potato raising, along with tourism, are the main economic sources. They also have a geothermal potential that portends a tremendous future.

Our plans called for a side trip to the Lava Beds so we head south on Hwy 39 towards Merrill, Malin, Tulelake, and the Lava Beds National Monument.

Driving along we pass evidence of centuries old violent volcanoes that spread molten masses of lava upon the level land and when the lava cooled, it created one of the most bewitching and interesting landscapes . . . cindercones. Out of these cones came dark, winding trenches that range for miles. These snake-like trenches can be 20 to 100 feet deep and 50 to 250 feet wide. Some of the caves have lava stalactites hanging from the ceiling or protruding from the wall sides.

Most of the caves are on the Cave Loop Road in the headquarters. Northwest of headquarters is the junction to the Merrill Ice Cave in which remains ice all year long. Skull Ice Cave has three levels and is one of the largest in the region going to 75' above the floor. It is called Skull Cave because so many skulls of Bighorn and Pronghorn were found. Detailed maps of various caves and how to find them are available at headquarters and it would take a full day to see most of the nearby trenches and caves. We had to pick and choose.

This area is also known as Captain Jack's Stronghold. The Modoc War of 1872-73 was probably one of the most costly in terms of number of Indians involved ever entered into by the United States. The Modocs became hostile when the settlers invaded the land of the Modocs near Tule Lake and Lost River. The Indians, however, finally agreed to move to the Klamath Indian Reservation with the exception of one small band led by Captain Jack who said no that it was Indian country. November, 1872, troops, aided by settlers, tried to force the Modocs onto the Reservation; however, in a short fight the Indians caused sufficient casualties to escape to the lava beds . . . now known as Captain Jack's Stronghold. While retreating, the Modocs murdered 14 male settlers at nearby ranches. In January 1873, soldiers and volunteers attacked the Indians' stronghold and ten percent of their number were killed. The Indians numbered some 70 fighting men and approximately 90 women, children, and elderly. In April, cut off by water and torn by dissention, the Modocs left their fortress and during the ensuing two months it was a running battle which ended on June 1 when Captain Jack was captured and hanged on October 3, 1893. The remainder of the band was moved to Oklahoma. The battlefields are practically the same today as in 1873.

About 250 species of plants grow in the area among the lava flows and many shades of green in junipers, ponderosa pine, flowering antelope bitterbush, mountain-mahogany, and wild current, dot the landscape. Purple sage, vivid scarlet painted cup or Indian paintbrush, pale blue wild flax make brilliant contrasts among the grays of the lava backdrop. There are about 40 species of mammals and old trails of Bighorn are still visible on some of the buttes. Some 200 species of birds inhabit the Lava Beds land.

We must be on our way. The ham and cheese sandwiches, hot coffee, and apple pie, eaten at one of the rest areas, was delicious.

On our return trip we retraced our route back on Hwy 39 to the junction of Hwy 140 east towards Lakeview. We pass towns named for people, battles, Indians . . . Dairy, Beatty, Bly. This is arid and desolate country. There are sagebrush, dwarf juniper trees, and miles of nothing . . . rimrocks and the wail of the coyote.

The little town of Bly, population probably about 100, is a logging town and there are cattle ranches in the area. There is a post office, (since 1873), grocery store, and tavern. But for the vacationer seeking solitude, turn off Hwy 140 a little east of Bly to the Mitchell Recreation Area and Gearheart

Mountain Wilderness. The road is full of curves and you may meet a logging truck doing double time towards you at any moment. Eventually, you will find Swede Cabin Flats. One can go on, at one's own risk, to Vee Pasture, but it takes a good car, and great hardiness. Of note . . . the ecosystem in this part of the West is so delicate and complex, the Forest Service has declared it a research natural area. Unfortunately, the one claim to world-wide attention for Bly, at Mitchell Recreation Area, is that six people were killed by a Japanese bomb during WWII while they were picnicking . . . May 5, 1945. It was the only place on the American continent where someone died as a result of enemy action during the war.

Leaving Bly and continuing on Hwy 140, I cross over Quartz Mountain, Grizzly Bear Peak, Drews Gap, and drop down into Langell Valley and the city of Lakeview. Much of the area from Dairy to Lakeview is uninhabited as it was when the pioneers on their way to the West and fertile farming soil crossed over it years ago.

Captain John Fremont's expedition passed through Lake County in December, 1843, in deep snow and howling winds. He named both Lake Abert and Abert Rim for his superior Col. J. J. Abert. At one time the lake is believed to have been the home of approximately 5,000 native Americans in small villages surrounding its shores. Abert Rim is said to be the largest exposed fault (about 30 miles long) on the North American Continent. There is the 70 foot deep remnant of a long ago earthquake, the Lost Forest, a mysterious ponderosa pine grove in the midst of the desert and Fort Rock caused by the collapse of a volcanic cone. Hart Mountain, rising above the fertile Warner Valley, is the home of a National Antelope Refuge and in the southernmost end of Lake County is Goose Lake bisected by the Oregon-California border.

We drove into Lakeview, checked our hotel accommodations, and then on to Goose Lake. This lake is also known as The Lake That Wasn't There. Jesse Applegate crossed the dry lake bed in 1846 with his wagon train. Goose Lake then filled with water and for about 80 years remained a lake, then dried up again. The wagon wheel tracks and horses' hooves of the early settler's crossing were plainly visible in the sand and silt. It is a weird and tricky body of water nestled in the Goose Lake Valley and is, at times, 20-28 miles long and 4-10 miles wide when filled.

At one time the lake's waves lapped at the doors of Lakeview some 14 miles away. In 1901, the Goose Lake Valley was considered a wonderful growing region for all temperate zone products. There was plenty of land and the railroad was aiming at it from two directions.

Fairport, CA., clung to the southeast shore of the shimmering lake . . . a mile away was the town of New Pine Creek, OR. Besides excellent farm and grazing land and abundant wild game in the early days, gold was discovered in nearby mountains. Some of the largest trout ever to be hooked came out of nearby Cave Lake. Fairport quickly became the fun and recreation center of the Goose Lake Valley and from 1908 to 1917 weekends at Fairport overflowed with revellers attending horse races, baseball, games, boating, dancing, family picnics and outings.

January 11, 1912, the Lakeview Examiner headlined "Railroad Day is major event . . . 300 people attend celebration." Blacksmiths, stables, stores, hotel/restaurants . . . prosperity abounded and the Fairport Inn was constructed on the shores of the then expanded Goose Lake. It was a modern, stylish piece of architecture complete with wood paneling, impressive stairway, a complement of 50 guest rooms and an immense ballroom that could accommodate 200 couples. The population of the town was about 900. From its veranda, the old steamer "Lakeview" could be seen crossing the lake. Unfortunately, the Inn was gutted by fire in 1930.

The question often asked by tourists when they view the waters of Goose Lake today is, "Did boats really ply the waters of Goose Lake when the deepest part is no more than 24 feet and much of the shore only waist high?" Yes. The most successful was the "Lakeview" which was 75' long, 18' wide, flat bottomed, double deckered and used for carrying passengers and freight. There was also a beauty called "Lady of the Lake" that moved about on the lake until 1919 when she was left high and dry during a freeze and the lake dropped its water level. Several small craft, used strictly for freight purposes, churned about on the waters but the shallow lake with the moving sand reefs and winds that blew continually, eventually played havoc with them all.

One pioneer recalled that Goose Lake went dry from 1931-34 and the blackweed grass came up so thick on the lake bed, they wintered their sheep on it. In the summer the silt and alkali dust were so thick that every time the wind blew people wore masks to cover their faces while doing outside chores or going about.

Goose Lake appeared in Ripley's "Believe It or Not" column in 1939 because of its constant disappearing act. Today, it is again with us, but for how long, who knows?

There were still many places to see but the sun had set, the clouds looked a little more like rain and we were tired and hungry. We stopped at the Lakeview Chamber of Commerce for more information on Lake County and then to the Lakeview Lodge Motel on North "G" Street. This was our first evening to choose rest before a leisurely dinner. We settled for a quick hamburger and fries and a glass of milk at the Indian Village Restaurant and retired to our room to study the Chamber's brochure and make plans for tomorrow.

How fortunate to live in a country that is so old and yet so young that a good part of its history is still in our time frame. Tonight our moon was hidden behind the clouds but it was just as well as we stayed awake only momentarily.

INDEX

NOTES:

Guide Six

The sixth day of our journey. The weather during this time has changed from cool and sunny on the coast, warm and sunny down the Columbia River, cool as we came down the high desert. Klamath Falls had brought some slumbering clouds, a little rain between the Lava Beds and Lakeview a light skift of moisture during the night. But, the morning brought a beautiful blue sky throughout the heavens. There was not a trace of a cloud to be seen.

We changed our clothes from heavy sweaters and pants to light cotton pants suit and we carried a light sweater, in case. We knew the farther south we drove the warmer it would get. We still wore our broken-in, broken-down walking shoes.

There would be few towns again on this morning's journey so we ate a good breakfast of bacon and eggs and the Indian Village Restaurant certainly gave substantial portions. Not knowing where we would be at lunchtime, we had sandwiches prepared, one thermos of coffee and one with lemonade.

We wanted to do some "poking" about in Lake County before beginning our southern route so headed towards Christmas Valley, Hwy 31. Whoever named it Lake County used the term rather loosely. One might picture lakes nestled amid stately evergreens and rugged peaks but that is not the case. The terrain was much the same as yesterday . . . wide open expanse, rimrocks, sagebrush. However, at this early hour the sagebrush had a bluish cast that almost matched the blue of the sky. It was almost impossible to determine where the sky and the land met. The sagebrush was in bloom and we took time to stop and "smell".

Many of the names throughout Lake County are the result of Captain John C. Fremont's expedition through that area in 1843. Summer Lake and Winter Ridge were named as he and his party reached the ridge in deep snow and howling winds only to see the sun shining and grass growing below.

We turned off at Valley Falls, drove by Lake Abert and Abert Rim, took the junction bringing us back through the Warner Lakes area and the Hart Mountain National Antelope Refuge. We were in luck. One of the pronghorn antelope, drinking cool morning waters, raised its head to gaze at us with its huge brown eyes looking straight into the camera. A magnificent animal.

47

Rabbit Hills, Coyote Hills, Blizzard Gap . . . Western ingenuity for naming this still somewhat frontier country. Within a 20-mile area surrounding Lakeview, Lake County offers fishing, camping, sawmill tours, golf, wild game hunting in season, skiing in season. The Schminck Memorial Museum in Lakeview houses one of the most unusual of pioneer life collections in Oregon. It is also a rockhound haven . . . Thunder Eggs, Hart Mountain Nodules, Fire Opal, Sunstones, and Petrified Wood. You can even try prospecting for gold.

But we must move on and we headed south on Hwy. 395. As we continued to pass miles of arid, waterless, desertlike countryside, we were reminded of a paragraph from the Bible, Isaiah, "The wilderness and the dry land shall be glad, the desert shall rejoice and blossom; like the crocus it shall blossom abundantly."

The car was getting low on gas, and we needed a cup of coffee, as we neared the town of Alturas, CA. The population is about 3500 and it is the county seat of Modoc County, incorporated in 1901. Alturas is 148 miles east of Redding, CA., 183 miles north of Reno, and 102 miles southeast of Klamath Falls, OR. The Modoc National Forest covers 69,500 acres in the Warner Mountains . . . Eagle Peak, 9906 feet; Warren Peak, 9722 feet; and Squaw Peak, 8650 feet. Here you will find Alpine scenery, peaks, canyons, glacial lakes, lush mountain meadows, trails for backpackers and horsemen. Fishing and hunting are good in season. During the spring and fall, Canadian geese and other waterfowl . . . Mallard, Teal, Gadwall, Wigeon, Pintail. Whistling swans number in the hundreds and you can see sandhill cranes, waterbirds, shorebirds and warblers dotting the landscape and heavens. Whitefronted geese are seen only in the spring. Six bald eagles have been known to winter here at one time. Mule deer, coyote, skunk, raccoon, mink, muskrat, ground squirrel, cottontail and black-tailed jackrabbit are year-round residents. Alturas is a small town and has probably remained about the same since its beginning but the size certainly does not determine the number of attractions to be found within Modoc County for the avid naturalist or the interested tourist.

Our coffee and buttered roll were gone and the car was impatient to be on its way. We moved on to Canby, just a spot in the road, Hwy 299, and then tackled the Adin Pass, elevation 5,173 feet. We had come from "the space where the

West still lives'' of wide open spaces, sage brush, wild animals of various species, and wilderness where no motor driven vehicle dared venture, to the abrupt change of tree covered mountains, streams, hidden lakes and cool, green ground cover of the Adin Pass country.

We picked a scenic meadow outside the town of Burney where a happy, meandering little creek flowed gently through green savanna alive with spring flowers to eat our meager but tasty sandwich. We slowly drank our coffee and lemonade and became one with the beauty of our surroundings.

This is hiker's country and Burney Falls a **must** for all those who can take the time to see this scenic waterfall. The countryside that encompasses Burney and Fall River Mills is almost a world apart from man.

Our drive today would be at a more leisurely pace. Once in Redding, we checked into the Red Lion Inn, took awhile to refresh ourselves and then drove northward on I-5 to Shasta Dam, Shasta Lake and some of the little historical towns lining the Interstate Highway.

The first stop . . . Shasta Dam. The tour was self guided but we took our time and read the statistics on the Dam and Lake Shasta. The Dam is the highest center overflow spillway dam in the world. At night the area is lighted and deer come out on the lawn to be fed by children and adults.

It is said, that one can go anywhere in America and never find an area with more diversity for outdoor lovers than that around Lake Shasta. Camping is permitted anywhere along the 370 mile shoreline. You could move your camp a mile each day for a year and never be in the same spot twice. On clear days, Mt. Shasta, considered by many as the most beautiful mountain in the world, provides a stunning backdrop for the lake. In the summer, waters are warmer than those off the ocean of Los Angeles. Because of the geographic location, Shasta Lake is ice-free the year around. There are no mosquitoes; pets are permitted. The U.S. Forest Service in Redding will provide a list of campgrounds and resort facilities.

Fishing . . . in season . . . in Shasta Lake offers bluegills, salmon, bass, trout, crappie, kamloops, catfish and sturgeon to name a few. Hunting is good for bear, squirrels, quail, wild pigeon, deer and doves. Elk hunting is permitted periodically.

Houseboating at Shasta Lake is one of the major recreations of the lake. There are several styles and price ranges. The marina has over 260 slips for covered moorage and row boats, fishing boats, ski boats, dinghies, canoes, zip sleds, wake riders for rent. You can also obtain water skis and tow ropes. There is plenty of room on Shasta's waters for everyone. As the resort was only 11 miles from Redding, we made reservations for dinner at the Bridge Bay Resort on our return trip that afternoon. While there, we also made reservations to see the Lake Shasta Caverns early the next morning.

Dunsmuir the "Historical Railroad Town" dates back to 1886. The present railroad route runs parallel to the Sacramento River, in many places offering train passengers scenic views from many angles. Each June the town celebrates "Railroad Days" wih a four day celebration. In the winter, there is ice fishing, snowmobiling, cross country skiing. We stopped at Mossbrae and Hedge Creek waterfalls and then drove through the Castle Crags State Park.

A few miles on is the town of Mt. Shasta nestled at the foot of the giant 14,162 foot mountain. For a small town it boasts a 26-acre city park located at Big Springs, the northernmost beginning of the Sacramento River. The Mt. Shasta area has some of the largest mule and black tail deer herds in California. The mountainous slopes, with their rocky points projecting above thick wooded and brushed areas, have proven ideal for the deer's habitat. There is also excellent bear hunting. Streams and lakes are innumerable for fishing and water enjoyment.

Mt. Shasta celebrates the Fourth of July with great vigor also . . . a parade, food and game booths, sidewalk sales, bicycle and foot races, car shows, baseball and horseshoe games, street dances, a barbeque and live entertainment at the City Park. All of this is topped off with a dessert of fireworks after dark. Christmas time brings Santa Claus in his sleigh touring the town to visit boys and girls for their Christmas happiness. The drive to the ski bowl is about 14 miles from the city and affords views of great grandeur. The 1980 census showed a population of 2800 people in the city and another 2700 in the surrounding valley. The principal industry is logging. The junction south of Mt. Shasta is the fastest route to Reno for travelers from the north.

Weed, approximately 12 miles north, is the junction for travelers going to Klamath Falls, OR via Hwy. 97 and those going on to Medford, OR via I-5. Weed was named after Abner Weed who came from the state of Maine and built a lumber mill. The mill, now owned by International Paper Company, is still the main community employer. Nearby is the two-year community college . . . College of the Siskiyous. A few miles off the highway is Lake Shastina, a rather large residential development.

Comfortable motel accommodations, in various price ranges, line the main streets of the triplet cities and a large variety of restaurants . . . American, Italian, Mexican, Chinese, serve the three cities of Weed, Dunsmuir, Mt. Shasta area.

Throughout our trip from Shasta Lake, the redbud bush, often called Judas Tree, was in full bloom. The crimson of its flowers against the pale green of the newly leafing trees, was a photographer's order of the day.

The sun had set in the mountains but when we reached the plateau of the Redding area and Shasta Dam, the last fading rays twinkled playfully over the blue waters. Boats of every description still moved about and the water skiers were too numerous to count.

Our reservations at the Bridge Bay Resort were in "Tail O' the Whale" Restaurant overlooking the lake and all of its activity. After sprucing up a bit, we were seated at a window table with a great view. We settled back with a cocktail and studied the menu which offered many mouth-watering suggestions. I opted for fresh salmon and my partner's choice was a filet mignon. We decided to celebrate our six day travels with a bottle of California Robert Mondavi . . . cabernet. The food, service, wine, and company were excellent. There were long periods of silence in our conversation as we watched an almost full moon, hanging gracefully over the bridge spanning I-5, a mile or so away, cast its golden rays across the silver lake.

We could tarry no longer or they would have charged us double for the space. It was Friday night, and as we entered Redding, we stopped at the Mt. Shasta Mall. There was a handicraft fair going on in the Mall which held our interest for some time. We visited several of the small businesses and left a fair amount of dollars for desired objects. We wished for more time to visit the Downtown Mall but time had run out.

We noted that Redding had a planetarium, community playhouse, theatre, museum, and art center. Five good-sized highways branch out of the Redding area taking one to almost any conceivable recreational pleasure desired. This is the heart of the Shasta Cascade *Wonderland* where opportunities for outdoor sport are literally unlimited. Redding has warm, sunny summers, and usually mild winters with only occasional mountain snows reaching the city floors. At the north end of Redding is one of the few places in America where you can see three large bridges within a mile.

We drove back to the Red Lion Inn along the Hilltop Drive Loop. The twinkling lights of the city on both sides could be seen for miles.

We felt a little nostalgia knowing that our journey was coming to an end but great pleasure over the enjoyment we had had, the country we had seen, the historical moments we had shared with some of its citizens, and the history we had viewed written in past pages of time.

We stopped at the lounge in the Red Lion for an after dinner drink, enjoyed the musical group and the dancers. We strolled leisurely back to our room, readied ourselves for retirement and pulled the drapes to let the moonlight enter our subconscious with all things good and beautiful.

INDEX

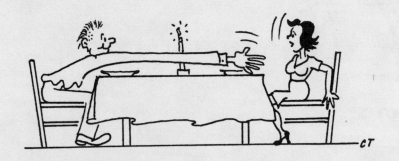

NOTES:

Guide Seven

Our seventh day and our circuit is almost complete. We have traveled the length and breadth of Oregon almost and the northern section of California. It has been a wonderful six day vacation so far and we plan to savor every bit of the journey to the end.

We headed for Lake Shasta Caverns a little after 7:00 a.m. It was another morning of unsurpassed beauty as we drove back towards Shasta Dam and located the Shasta Caverns dock for the 20-minute boat ride to the Chalet headquarters. There are three tours daily and we chose the early one. We boarded the catamaran and cruised Shasta's blue waters. Tree covered, majestic mountains, still untouched by the early rays of the morning sun, cast a regal spell of purple velvet over their dense forests. Still suspended on the horizon was the luminous, full moon.

A specially equipped bus awaited its passengers for the more than 800 foot drive above the lake surface. The drive was winding and narrow but the constant changing panorama of scenery in every direction afforded photographs of extraordinary beauty.

Inside, the caverns were iridescent in color. This is caused by the action of water on limestone and marble which has also carved huge, multi-colored columns as high as 60 feet. The walls are adorned with symmetrical folds of stone draperies and the white stalactite and stalagmite formations looked like brilliant crystals glittering in the artificial light.

Recordings of old Wintu Indian lore show that the natural wonder of the caverns was known to them since antiquity, but the first white explorer to find the caves was James A. Richardson, employee of the Federal Fisheries. Using carbide from his miner's lamp, he carved the date November 3, 1878, on the cavern wall. The notation is still legible. As we moved freely up and down the paved walks, stairs, and held on to the handy guard rails, we realized it was not always like this. The guide told us it was only in 1964 that visitors, as such, began visiting the caverns. Improvements have been added every year since that time. Coming back into the bright sunlight, we felt like Alice in Wonderland emerging from her underground fairyland.

It was past noon by the time we arrived back on I-5. We were hungry, but decided this time we would wait until we put a few miles behind us before indulging in one of our favorite pastimes . . . eating. At Redding, we took Hwy. 299 and headed the 150 miles toward Eureka, CA., through and over the famed Trinity Alps.

We drove slowly through Old Shasta, seven miles from Redding. Old Shasta was the end of the wagon road from the south in the 1850's and the leading gold mine center of the north. Receipts of $100,000 per week were claimed at one time. When the railroad went into the City of Redding, Old Shasta's days were doomed. It has been preserved as a Historical Monument since 1950. Our next trip through this area, we would plan to stop and look about the town which rings with the echoes of its past and still plays host to large numbers of visitors, interested in their American heritage, each year.

Whiskeytown Lake, with a small shoreline of 36 miles and a depth of 264 feet, was a short distance on. Picnic and camping sites, all near the beach, line the shore and the lake is considered good for the fishermen but the waters are cold. Some hardy swimmers will brave the icy waters as the water temperature climbs a few degrees in the summertime.

Our hunger was too much. As we came to the turnoff to French Gulch, we knew it was time to take a "food break". We would eat as well as tour this old-time town. It was Saturday and the restaurant opened at 10:30 a.m. We ordered scampi. It was excellent. Hunger pangs assuaged, we read the history of the little town of French Gulch while drinking our coffee.

It was settled by Canadians from Oregon in 1849. They found gold in the mountains and immediately named the community Morrowtown. But Morrowtown lacked lustre and it was renamed French Gulch. The area's first quartz mines opened in the 1850's. In 1855, a thousand miners were living in the area, supplies came in by ox teams, the average miner made from $100 to $200 a day and spent it freely.

The hotel, set on flat rocks, was built in the early 1800's by the Feeney family who traveled from Ireland to Trinity County. Unfortunately, as time passed, the hotel became a haunt for bootleggers and was eventually closed down as were the mines. A local story is still circulated about a bartender who once killed a customer because he got tired of hearing his same old jokes. The bartender was immediately hanged.

Before getting back into the car, we visited Fox's General Store owned by the same family for over 100 years. The

Oddfellows Hall is a classic example of Western simplicity in architecture.

Back on Hwy 299, and feeling much better, with a mixture of good food and history of our ancestors in the vicinity, we turned toward Weaverville. We had read a great deal about the old Chinese Temple built in the center of town and it was a **must stop**. It is called the Temple of the Forest and Clouds which is inscribed in Chinese characters above the door. Built in 1852, gutted by fire in 1873, it was rebuilt and completed in 1875. The carved altar is covered with pictures, statues of immortals, candles, and incense sticks. On one side hangs a spirit-summoning gong and drum. On the other, are exquisite examples of early handsewn robes. Some of these used the so-called "forbidden stitch". This stitching was prohibited after a number of the women went blind while doing the fine handiwork. The temple has been in continuous use since it was built. One local family, whose grandfather contributed to its building, still worship there.

*"Of the five great wildlands of the Klamath Mountains, only one has a truly national reputation. Such recognition is not perhaps in all ways an advantage, but there is no question that the landscape deserves it. This best-known area, also the largest of the five, is the 600,000 acre region of wilderness known as the Trinity Alps. Here is the largest block of wild country in California outside the Sierra Nevada, and, perhaps, without even that exception, the most varied. The name "Trinity Alps" can be properly applied to only one section of this many-branched mountain mass . . . a high dramatic core near the eastern edge. The northern slopes of these central alps are white most of the year with unmelting snow; there is even a miniscule glacier under the north face of Thompson Peak. Because of various and varied rock formations, they are broken down into three great regions . . . Red Trinities to the southeast, White Trinities to the northeast, and Green Trinities to the west. It is claimed to contain the largest area of uncut diversified forest in the Klamath Mountains." *Reprinted from *Home of Bigfoot Country* by John Hart©1975 by the Sierra Club . . . Reprinted by permission of Sierra Club Books.

We take our time to drive this wilderness delighting in the beauty every turn of the road brings into view. Mr. Hart's book, noted above, comments that "many small clear streams, running all year, are tributaries of Dot Creek. Along the watercourses grow low bushes of the mountain heath called kalmia (not the same as the rare *Kalmiopsis Leachinana* found only in one tiny corner of Oregon) which is also called American laurel and carries pink five-petaled flowers in season. The woods on top include Brewer spruce and noble fir seldom found south of the Klamath River." This too must be a next trip experience . . . and I plan to traverse some of the area by foot.

We had dallied and it was mid-afternoon as we came down the Trinity Alps into the farming community of and around Arcata. We had two uncompleted goals that must be achieved before the day's end. One, a visit to the Samoa cookhouse which is four minutes south of Eureka on Humbolt Bay and the other to visit the small town of Ferndale nearby.

In the early logging operations in the redwood country, the cookhouse served as the hub of the community. "Come and get it" was a familiar cry heard by the mill workers and it has since become an American home slogan. When the quitting time whistles blew, the men were ready to down a big meal and even the big, white horses that drew the lumber carts, knew the meaning of the whistles. They stopped in their tracks and refused to move until harnesses were unbuckled and they could head for their oats.

According to legend, and it wasn't very romantic, lumbermen worked six days a week, twelve hours a day for one dollar a day. A fraction of this dollar went for the three hot meals served daily. By 1922, the men were earning more and they paid 60 cents for three generous meals. Tables were and still are set "family style". Food was rarely passed and the "boarding house reach" came into being. The menu consisted of meat, potatoes, gravy, vegetables, bread baked in the cookhouse kitchen with fresh butter from the company's dairy, usually followed by cake, pie or fruit.

Bakers, using huge pots, beat eggs, added milk, sugar and vanilla. This was used to moisten dry ingredients along with shortening. The kids found it so good, they called it "egg-nog".

Until 1915, only single women were employed, but after that married women were occasionally hired. Waitresses worked seven days a week for five weeks before earning a day off. They received $30 a month and room and board. Each waitress was assigned to four tables, ten men to a table. As many as ten waitresses were employed regularly. Waitresses came in at 6:00 a.m. and worked until 7:00 p.m. except in the summer when it was 9:00 p.m.

There were no reserved seats, but some of the men had been there so long, no one dared to sit in "their" place. The splintery wooden floors, scarred by the calked boots of the pondmen, were scrubbed every Thursday. Everyone, except the boss, was provided with a husky broom and a plentiful supply of soapy water and "had at it".

Today the Samoa Cookhouse, the last surviving cookhouse in the West, continues the tradition of serving lots of good food, family style. We had dinner after touring the area and going through the museum which shows early culinary items in addition to historical mementos from the early years of logging and lumbering industries.

Although we were going no farther south on Hwy. 101, the tourist coming north or going south, with or without children, should plan a stop to ride the "Super Skunk Train". It operates out of Fort Bragg and Willets. The trip takes approximately two hours and reservations should be made ahead of time in the summer months. The train goes through the heart of the Boulevard of Redwoods which is inaccessible to automobiles. Fort Bragg is 142 miles south of Eureka and about 166 miles from San Francisco north. The railroad was originally operated by the Union Lumber Company of Fort Bragg as a logging railroad. The railcars are called "Skunks" because local people always said you could smell them before you could see them. Passenger service was started in 1925. Spacious windows line both sides of the railroad cars providing wonderful visibility for sightseers . . . especially the children. In 1965, the California Western Railroad added an authentic oldtime passenger train called "Super Skunk" and it is a regularly scheduled, standard gauge steam train.

The sun was setting as we checked into the Red Lion Inn at Eureka. Ferndale, 15 miles out of Eureka, still had to be visited. We found it a "jackpot" of well-kept pioneer homes, businesses, and neighborly friendliness.

Ferndale was settled in August 1852, when Seth and Stephen Shaw sank their roots into Eel River valley soil. These men borrowed an Indian log canoe to travel across the North Bay of Eel River on up Salt River to the junction of a small creek to be known later as Francis Creek. There they cut a path through the dense thicket where ferns stood six feet high and their diary states, "after four days of severe labor . . . have got a passable road through the timber."

The initial turning point in Ferndale's deterioration began in a general restoration of all the homes and buildings in

1973. According to a newspaper article of that year, "Today, one may see fine examples of the over-all refurbishing and restoration of Ferndale in the beautifully coordinated colors of the homes and businesses that make the streets come alive. Ferndale has been reborn."

Ferndale has a wealth of homes dating from 1860-1915 varying in styles from Carpenter-Gothic, Victorian-Gothic, Eastlake Stick, Queen Anne to the modern.

The Gumdrop Tree House was most unique and distinctive, and to my knowledge, matchless. It was built in 1875, by Mr. A. Berding, merchant, and is still owned and lived in by his descendants. His store stood close by as well as a Berding owned warehouse across the street which is now the Danish Hall. The name Gumdrop Tree House originated because of the carefully trimmed cypress trees in front which resemble giant gumdrops and they are an "eye-full". I have pictures to prove it.

Two interesting articles taken from the 1894 Ferndale paper noted that "William Holland, who hails from Table Bluff, was found by Officer Bulekeley late Saturday night acting queerly on "E" Street. Holland seemed to have more money than he thought necessary to finish the night and was trying to get rid of some of it by scattering it on the sidewalk in front of the Bank of Eureka. Holland and his money were picked up and taken to the lock up, and yesterday morning his surplus cash was reduced by $6.00." "Disturbed Congregation. The person who disturbed the congregation last Sunday by continually coughing is requested to buy a bottle of Foley's Honey and Tar."

Ferndale plays host to some 10,000 people who attend Ferndale's Art Festival each May, held the week before Mother's Day, and the highlight of the event is the Kinetic Sculpture Race. Other traditional celebrations are the Memorial Day Parade, Portuguese Holy Ghost Parade in the spring, Scandinavian Festival in June and annual antique show held in September sponsored by the Chamber of Commerce. The old Hart Theatre has been remodeled into the Village Theatre and Ferndale Little Theatre presents professional legitimate theatre productions in the winter and spring.

When we returned to the Red Lion Inn, we ordered a bottle of champagne, bathed, got into some relaxing clothes and spent a most enjoyable evening musing over our vacation of a lifetime.

At the beginning we had been rather timid about traveling alone, concerned about accommodations, people's reception in the towns and cities of the places visited, but doubt and fear had been conquered as it usually is if you dare to try. The people throughout both states had met us with great friendliness and were eager to provide us with information about themselves, their lifestyles, their communities. Coming back to Eureka through the **Avenue of Giant Redwoods** was a perfect ending.

Our vacation, in every sense of the word, had become a treasure chest of learning and enjoyment. While few things, including vacations, are perfect, this had been about as close to perfection as one could have anticipated. I had left my comb and tooothbrush in one motel, forgotten to tip an especially outstanding waiter at one restaurant, almost run out of gas with no station for 25 miles, but then, que sera. I bought another comb and toothbrush. I sent a tip to the management to be delivered to Ron, and I found gas at a local farmer's to get me into the next town.

Mellow with champagne and the moon winking at me from the corner of the window, I laid my head on the comfortable pillow and a thousand ideas rushed through my head for my next, yet unknown, vacation through another part of the wonderful western United States.

INDEX

NOTES:

Guide Eight

The Oregon pioneer had to be hardy, determined, gregarious, persistent, and perceptive in order to survive. The spirit is still prevalent. It was the "betting" spirit that brought about the name of Portland . . . it is common knowledge that had the flip of the coin been different, it would have been called Boston.

Portland, Oregon, was born in "Old-Town" and its rebirth was kindled there. Today, after several years of resolute restoration, Old-Town is zinging with new businesses, good restaurants, a nightlife including stage show revues, and plays in the newly refurbished Storefront Theatre. Each Saturday and Sunday, April through Christmas, Portland sponsors a Saturday Market held beneath the Burnside Bridge. Various artists and vendors proudly display their handmade products and sell them direct to customers. The Portland City Police Department has a Bicentennial Museum on NW 2nd. Old-Town contains several landmarks which Portlanders point to with pride—the Skidmore Fountain, a favorite meeting site about 1880 and the Bickel Building on SW Ash, which held the town's first soda fountain. Chinatown is also in the Old-Town vicinity and the Portland Chinatown community was the second largest in the United States in 1890. This area is designated a National Historic Landmark District and the best way to see, touch and feel the nostalgia of the past and present is to walk it. I did. The Visitor's Information Center provided me with maps and attractions to see along the way.

The 33rd state to enter the Union in 1859, Oregon offers great diversity in climate and topography. From the rain forests, heavily forested mountains, rivers and fertile valleys of the western part to the arid and harsh climate of the eastern deserts, visitors see such natural wonders as the vast Pacific Ocean bordering the west, the Columbia River Gorge in the north, Oregon Caves and Crater Lake in the south, and the "moon country" of Central Oregon. The eastern border between Oregon and Idaho is formed partly by the winding Snake River and Hells Canyon, the deepest gorge on the North American continent. The City of Portland and surrounding area is one of lush vegetation, fertile soil, and water . . . rivers, lakes, creeks, falls. The heartland of Oregon is contained in the Willamette Valley which includes the cities of Portland, Salem, and Eugene.

Towns, cities, clothes, food, and tools are only a few of the things named after Indian words and tribes. At one time 125 Indian tribes populated the territory of Oregon some of which included the Chinook, Tillamook, Yamel, Molaha, Clackamas, Multnomah, Santiam, Coos, Cayuse, Northern Piaute, Umatilla, Nez Perce, Bannock, Klamath, and Modoc. The Canoe Indians, of the Columbia River, were well known for their outstanding log canoes.

Portland, also known as the City of Roses, marked its Diamond Jubilee celebration of the annual tournament in 1983. The ten day festival held in June culminates in a grand floral parade. Roses cover the floats, the city, the countryside, the parks, the fair where judging is held for thousands of excited rose growers who know their "rose" will be the winner.

Portland is split by the Willamette River with the older section on the west side. This part houses the downtown business district, many of its bigger parks, and a good number of its residents who have beautiful homes on the mountainside with magnificent views. On the east side are the airport, Memorial Coliseum, Lloyd Shopping Center and main residential area. A leisurely driving tour of both sides of the Willamette will take the better part of a day.

Literally "alive" with parks, Portland has little parks, big parks, parks of roses, parks of azaleas, plain park blocks with all kinds of greenery. To name a few of the some 160 parks throughout the Portland area, there are Washington Park, Forest Park, Pettygrove Park, Waterfront Park, Wooded Macleay Park, Council Crest Park, Duniway Park, Terwilliger Boulevard Park, and Tryon Creek State Park. I stopped at the Visitor's Information Center across from Waterfront Park, on Salmon Street and picked up sightseeing information for the city . . . its parks and its museums.

The Tri-Met transportation system on SW Yamhill Street provided me with a copy of "Portland Mall Walk" as well as bus schedules and transported me to any place in the Multnomah, Washington, Clackamas, Oregon counties, and Vancouver, Washington, served by the Tri-Met 75 bus lines. Busses arrive and leave from downtown areas on 5th and 6th Avenues with passengers riding free if they are going within the "Fareless Square" area. Busses stop at all city parks, museums, gardens, and many other places of general interest within the designated area. The fare is nominal and you can leave the driving to the expert while you relax, sightsee and ask questions of the local, friendly residents.

The Tri-Met system provides covered shelters and the seven regional areas served by the company are given a color and a symbol. Symbols are placed on the shelters to identify the shelter with the busses stopping there. The shelters contain a large map of the system and a computerized video screen where, just by pushing a button, passengers' questions can be answered.

An interesting little aside . . . in the 1850's two downtown blocks were donated to the city . . . one was used by men only and the other by women only. Beautiful Elk Fountain still separates these blocks but discrimination is out and "use" is in. Now both genders together or separately, enjoy the green blocks.

One of the busiest ports on the West Coast, Portland's port includes the largest floating dry dock. Walkways are on all the bridges except Marquam and Fremont allowing the tourist and native alike to view the excitement that always surrounds a busy waterway. While port watching, I was fortunate to view the old "Portland" paddle wheel steamer which it is said, may be one of the last of its kind in the world.

Taking a rail-cruise tour through the Columbia Gorge, is a trip I plan to repeat. With a small picnic basket, I boarded Amtrak's "Pioneer" and rode to Cascade Locks. I then transferred to the Columbia Sightseer for a two hour narrated cruise which was informative and fun. This is about a half day tour from Portland so that you have plenty of time to roam around on your own, either before or after the cruise, and visit the museum. To be sure of a seat during the tourist months, you should probably make arrangements at least a few days ahead of your anticipated trip.

John's Landing, another of Portland's restored historical landmarks, is one of the oldest industrial areas. Now there are specialty shops, restaurants, offices, and the original water tower still stands forth atop the building.

Must stop . . . The old Pittock Mansion. Newspaper tycoon Henry Pittock built the elegant, French Renaissance style mansion 1909-14. The architecture is tasteful and luxurious . . . reminiscent of that period. The mansion provides an elevator, telephones to all rooms, and a central cleaning system. One can tour the grounds without charge but a small fee is asked for touring the inside.

Must stop . . . Washington Park overlooks the City of Portland and is set on terraced slopes . . . The International

Rose Test Gardens are ablaze with glory in June when more than 8000 rose bushes are in bloom. There is also a Japanese Garden covering five acres of wooded area with cherry trees vying for top honors as they blossom abundantly, delicately, perfuming the April air. Also in the park is the Western Museum of Science and Industry, the zoo, and Western Forestry Center. Next to Washington Park is the Hoyt Arboretum where an avid botanist could "go bananas" for days.

Must stop . . . The Sanctuary of Our Sorrowful Mother, off 82nd and Sandy Boulevard, should be a standard prescription for today's stress patient. This quiet, tranquil, serene, and restful Grotto offers outdoor masses on Sundays, May through September, and an elevator will whisk you to the nearby cliff-top for more tranquitlity, more landscaped gardens, and a memorable view of the Columbia River.

Must . . . if the time of the year is right . . . The Oregon Museum of Science and Industry, holds its Epicurean Experience where more than 30 restaurants and Oregon wineries put on a tasting party for hundreds of guests.

Must stop . . . Oregon City, only a few miles out of Portland, should be a definite goal of Portland visitors. John McLoughlin of the Hudson Bay Company settled the site in 1843 and it was the first territorial capital. The first Oregon newspaper, *The Oregon Spectator*, was published in Oregon City in 1846. It was the first newspaper west of the Mississippi River. As the city is built next to a cliff, there is an elevator to lift pedestrians the 90 some feet up from the river to the cliff's residential sections of the city. Oregon City, too, has joined the long list of Historical Monuments of Oregon and it is well deserved.

Must, if possible, visit Sauvie Island. It is said that for centuries this island was a summer and autumn home to the Multnomah Indians. It is the largest island in the Columbia and was named after a Hudson Bay Company employee named Sauve. It is considered a Portland suburb with superb summer recreational actitivites . . . swimming, boating, and picnicking. It is also a game management area for wintering waterfowl. It still retains an aura of pastoral beauty and it is worth the extra time to visit.

If you are going the south end of Mt. Hood, follow the Sam Barlow, early pioneer, trail. He was the first to conquer this route that others feared to tread. When he started out, Barlow said, "God never made a mountain but that he provided a place for man to go around it." Deep gashes still show on the trunks of trees along the old Barlow route where ropes were used to slow the descent of the wagons, but around it they went and the majority survived.

Oregon was linked with the rest of the United States by rail in 1883 and the economic growth in forestry and agriculture began booming. In the early 1900's, most of the people lived in a rural setting but by the closing years of the 21st century, a switch had occurred with the majority of the population becoming urbanites. However, in the sparsely populated eastern central area, it is not uncommon for ranches to exceed 1500 acres.

There are so many things to do, to see, to experience, to learn, to accomplish . . . so many people to talk with . . . we have only covered a thin surface. A stay of three days would be suggested to really relish the paradise of Portland.

Sport shows, expositions, operas, symphonies, theatres, arts-craft shows, festivals, specific events change daily and information of present and coming attractions can be obtained from the Portland Chamber of Commerce or State Tourist Information Bureau. The Chamber of Commerce will provide you with listings of good motels/hotels/inns, dining facilities, maps, and current prices.

There is a wide range of choice, depending on what area of the city you will be doing most of your traveling, sightseeing, or shopping. If you wish to be near Lloyds's Center, east side, there is the tastefully luxurious Red Lion Inn across the street from the Center. The Red Lion Inn or Thunderbird at Jantzen Beach are only a few minutes from Washington on I-5. The Red Lion Inn at Portland Center on the west side of the Willamette gives you city access. The Red Lion Inn at the Coliseum on the east side, called "the Motherbird Inn", is a particular favorite of Red Lion's travelers. The Red Lion/Thunderbird chain is noted for its quality in every respect.

Portland is a resplendent city, and a tribute to all those hardy, tenacious pioneers such as Sam Barlow who decided the Oregon Territory was one of the best places in the United States to "call home".

INDEX

THIS IS FUN?

NOTES:

Guide Nine

Eugene is only 115 miles from Portland, and I am sure the traveler will question why such a short distance in one day. Again, there is so much to see and do in Oregon and the Willamette Valley is a grand area providing many choices.

This part of Oregon has a long season of colorful foliage and it is reflected in the wide variety of hues among the trees, shrubs, ground cover. Spring is a particularly delightful time of the year to travel this part of the Pacific Northwest and watch nature's magic unfolding of new leaves on budding trees, baby green fronds of ferns projecting from the warm earth, moss renewing its youthful color, and flowering shrubs and wild flowers covering field and mountainside.

Trying to work my time into my travel options, I left Portland about 7:30 a.m. As I had already seen Oregon City in **Guide Eight**, I took I-5, but for those who have not been to Oregon City, do so, via old Highway 205.

Note of interest . . . Jesse Applegate was given authority to replat the city of Oregon City, making it larger than the original Moss survey. He used a rope four rods long instead of the usual surveyor' s chain, and the variation in the rope's length due to moisture conditions and stretching accounts for the irregular size of the Oregon City lots.

My first exit was to Champoeg State Park. It was at Champoeg that the Willamette settlers, May 2, 1843, voted to establish a provisional government and become free of the British Hudson Bay Company rule. It was a close vote, 50-52, but the valley became the first such government on the Pacific Coast.

At that time, Champoeg was a busy shipping point but later was destroyed by floods. It is difficult to imagine now, but at one time, the Willamette River had a colorful riverboat past with ships traversing the river daily from Portland to Eugene.

Leaving the visitor center at Champoeg, I took the French Prairie Loop, a 40 mile back country journey on good roads. I stopped briefly at St. Paul, now a historic district, and then turned on the east side of the loop into the towns of Woodburn, Aurora and Canby. Aurora started as a religious community in 1856 and many treasures remain in the Aurora Ox Barn Museum.

I doubled back about 16 miles to the Tigard exit #294, off I-5. I wanted to make sure I saw Champoeg, but I also wanted to start at Tigard and go through Newberg to Salem via 99W.

This is some of the richest farmland country in Oregon. Many farmers made small fortunes during the years 1850-1870 and the results of their success are seen in some of the still beautifully maintained, handsome houses set among picturesque farm country. Unfortunately, I assume, because of the expense of present day upkeep, many of the houses are in need of repair or are past repair and should be razed. I drove without haste to Salem.

Covered bridges dot the countryside throughout the northern section of Oregon. The first covered bridge, I learned, was built across the Taulity River near Hillsboro circa 1850. I also raised the question as to why bridges were covered and learned it was to keep the wood from rotting, protect the trusses, and keep the snow off the bridge.

From 1830 on, thousands of Americans migrated to the Pacific Northwest and in 1834 Salem was founded by Methodist missionaries. About nine years later, Oregon representatives organized their provisional government at Champoeg and patterned their laws after those of Iowa. A year later, the British government abandoned its hold on Oregon country and moved to Ft. Victoria.

When the territorial legislature met at Oregon City in 1851, they decided on Salem for the capital. However, there were a few who opposed this move from Oregon City but to Salem they went in 1852. The legislature, dissatisfied with the unfinished buildings and cramped quarters, voted to move the capital to Corvallis in 1855. However, Congress had appropriated money for the erection of a capitol and other public buildings at Salem and refused to recognize the Corvallis site for the state government . . . Salem remained the capital.

Oregonians are extraordinarily proud of their structure of government and Oregon has been the innovator of many new legislative concepts. The initiative and referendum were introduced in 1902 and the voters themselves are able to initiate and vote on new laws, old laws, and constitutional changes. They instituted a system of recall for inefficient, unqualified elected officials. Oregon was one of the earliest states to start a state income tax . . . 1923.

I wanted to spend as much time as possible in the Capitol and the Capitol Mall. The Capitol is a beauty. Events in Oregon history are depicted in wall murals and sculptures. The polished bronze state seal glows directly under the dome. On top of the white marble capitol dome is a 24 foot Pioneer statue done in gold leaf. You can even climb the 121 spiral steps to the tower should you feel inclined. The Mall was ablaze with springtime beauty. Travel information about Salem or the state can be obtained at the Oregon Tourism Bureau in the Mall offices.

After the Capitol visit, I drove to the historic Bush home which belonged to the first Salem newspaper publisher and banker. It still contains many of the family's furnishings. The barn on the estate has been turned into an art center and is open to the public. There are 89-acres of formal and natural wildflower landscaping. I drove to the Deepwood Estate and it, too, is well kept both inside and out.

Just east of the Capitol Mall are two of the Pacific Northwest's oldest houses . . . the home of Jason Lee the missionary leader and the Methodist parsonage. Both are available for touring.

If your interest happens to be yarn-making, visit the old Thomas K. Woolen mill and warehouse. The antique machinery is on display. If you desire to go on to Stayton, there is a guided tour through the Paris Woolen Mill. Built in 1905, the Paris Mill is the oldest fully operating woolen mill in the state.

Tourists visiting the state during fair time should plan at least an extra half day, more if possible, to see the exhibits and old-fashioned fair entries. The Oregon State Fairgrounds are the 18th largest fairgrounds in North America.

Willamette University was next on my priorities. It is the oldest in the West . . . 1842. I stopped briefly at the Reed Opera House whose four stories now include shops, restaurants, and offices.

Considering myself a budding wine connoisseur, I drove to Honeywood Winery, one of Oregon's oldest wineries (1934) and stopped for some wine testing. While most of Oregon's wines are young, they are promising.

Of interest . . . in choosing a name for the "town" of Salem, which had one house when it was platted, the Calapooya Indian name "Chemeketa" or "place of rest" was proposed, but the missionary preferred a Biblical word so they chose "Salem" with a similar meaning.

Salem area has 40 developed parks, over 35 regulation tennis courts, over 100 lakes, campsites, picnic areas, and historical markers. In the fall, there is excellent salmon and steelhead fishing along the coast which is about an hour's drive from Salem. Streams and lakes in the Cascades provide trout fishing in the summer. Warm water fishing is available in ponds and backwater areas along the Willamette River. **For children only . . . Mill Creek in Salem may be fished in season.**

Before leaving Salem, I stopped for a quick sandwich and cup of tea. I wasn't sure how long it would be before the opportune time came again.

The Enchanted Forest south of Salem . . . a beautiful world of fantasy is blended into a natural setting of lush vegetation. There is an admission fee which is nominal and it is open from March through September . . .a **must** for both adults and children.

Water lovers . . . ferries . . . there are several in the backcountry still crossing the Willamette River. The old-fashioned, cable-drawn boats allow grand views of the wide, tranquil, sometimes turbulent river. The northernmost ferry is out of Canby about 25 miles south of Portland on US 99E. If you stop at Champoeg State Park, take the ferry trip if at all possible. The river here is quiet and clear and you can spend the time daydreaming of past and present. Wheatland Ferry runs from Newberg and Salem. It is a busy little ferry and probably the most historic. The first mission post in Oregon was built on the east bank and the homes lining the river on the east side are about 100 years old. Lincoln Ferry on Oregon Hwy. 221 is swathed in steamboat landing lore. The Buena Vista Ferry northwest of Albany, once a busy landing, is now reduced to haunting memories but allows melodious views of the river and countryside. All these ferries can be reached in a day and still allow for historic and scenic stops between.

More water fun . . . take exit 194 near Eugene . . . Autzen Stadium sign. You can canoe from Alton Baker Park to Springfield about 2.5 miles. Canoes can be rented at several places in Eugene. This is also a lovely spot for a picnic and there is a fascinating children's playground and contemporary sculpture.

Eugene is the site of the University of Oregon and of Northwest Christian College. It is also the cultural and industrial center of the upper Willamette Valley. The Willamette River curves around the northwest quarter of the city through fields, wooded hills, leaning groves of cottonwood and balm . . . eastward is the mighty and towering Cascade Range and westward the misty summits of the Coast Range.

Eugene F. Skinner built a crude log cabin at the foot of a small peak in 1846, and there his young wife gave birth to the first child born in Lane County. The peak was called Skinner's Butte and here the first Post Office in the region was established. Skinner started a ferry near the present Ferry Street Bridge, he dabbled in real estate and, with Judge Risdon, platted a townsite in 1852.

There are several choices for viewing the splendiferous scenery surrounding this part of the valley. There is the Mohawk Loop through the Mohawk Valley which is about a two hour drive and the Lorane Loop, also a couple hours trip through the beautiful Coast Range valleys to Lorane. Clear Lake Loop for mountain lovers is about five hours. This drive passes through white water, falls, lakes, and immense timber. Take a camera. The Ocean Loop is another four-five hour trip going through the Coast Range but if you have missed the coast it will bring you out at Heceta, Sea Lion Caves, and great eye-filling ocean views . . . the other direction, the sand dunes, campgrounds, and beaches. It is said there are about 21 covered bridges along the McKenzie-Eugene area . . . Highway 126.

My driving time was still early afternoon so I decided on what I called the **"Breath-taker Loop"**. I took Highway 126 east through Springfield to Highway 242. The road wandered through gigantic evergreens of cedar, douglas fir, sugar pine, hemlock, past Blue River and at the top a panoramic view of the snow-capped peaks of the Cascades awaited me.

The Willamette Valley presents a picture of tidy, white houses and church spires nestling by the Willamette River. It is almost like a transplant from a New England town with its touching and graceful pastoral scenes.

I admit that by the hour of my return to Springfield, I was grateful to see the Red Lion Motor Inn sign directly off I-5. Upon checking in, I made reservations in the dining room. While I would almost have preferred to have ordered soup and sandwich in my room, I didn't want to miss any opportunity to meet and talk with other travelers or hometown people. For those wanting to drive a few more miles to Eugene and perhaps get an early start seeing the city or shopping, there is a Red Lion/Thunderbird Motor Inn on Coberg Road.

Tomorrow morning I planned to tour the University of Oregon campus, museum of art on the campus which is famous for its Oriental art collection, check out some of the

City's craft shows, and be on my way to find the "**Lost Mines of Bohemia**" 20 miles south of Cottage Grove. I would recommend that everyone take the Village Green exit off I-5 and ride the Goose Train. It, too, goes into the Bohemia Mine country. It is a super experience and while I have ridden it twice and look forward to another time, this trip I had other priorities. The Goose Train got its name during pre-WWI days when it lurched and bucked over rough track as it brought down its loads of logs from the high forest. It leaves about 2 p.m. and returns about 5 p.m.

Addendum on Corvallis, Oregon

The college town of Corvallis, halfway between Eugene and Salem, provides a beautiful drive through lush farming country, past green trees, greener vegetation, emerald waters, over the Mary's and Willamette Rivers and around, beneath, over and through covered bridges. One could go to Corvallis out of Salem and emerge at Eugene or take 99W and get a good look at this part of the valley.

The Benton County Courthouse is the oldest Oregon courthouse still in use. Even though a modern wing has been added, the old tower clock sits proudly over the cupola.

Stop at the Thompson Feed Mill in the Corvallis-Albany area on the banks of the Calapooya River. Built in 1862, it is on the National Register and tours are given the third weekend of the month.

Corvallis, one of the older cities in the state, has many historic buildings, monuments, markers, antique shops and **a must** is the Cannery Mall. Look around and see their unique architecture and visit their shops . . . stop for a sandwich or a cool drink. The original cannery was a major contributor to the local economy. The Mall, which is fully enclosed, has more than 20 shops, stores, restaurant, lounge, and a delicatessen. There is plenty of parking and it is easily accessible from the main street going into Corvallis.

There is a wealth of campgrounds, picnic areas, fishing, rockhounding, bicycling, and swimming in and around Corvallis.

Don't forget to stop and enjoy the outstanding rest stops off I-5 as you feel the need for lunch breaks, potty stops, walking the dog, or relaxing from the strain of driving. Oregon is to be commended for these pretty, well-kept *Treat* stops for all travelers.

78

INDEX

NOTES:

Guide Ten

Another full day loomed ahead. I was up at 5:30 and ready to leave at 7:00 a.m. I find the early morning hours invigorating, relaxing, and stimulating in getting the mental juices working. With all the exciting places to stop and visit, there were going to be some hard choices.

While breakfasting, I noted that Lane County has 157 parks and forest camps . . . 60 with tent sites, 33 trailer sites, 105 with water and restrooms . . . 101 picnic facilities. There is fishing, water sports, hiking trails, bicycling, horseback riding and no end of historic skeletons (both buidings and human) in the area.

I did not take the guided campus tour at the University of Oregon as it was too early but with my trusty map, I found most of the buildings I wanted to see. I was fortunate enough to find the Museum of Art building open and had a quick, special tour given me by the kind gentleman who was there so early and who obviously had a great background in his subject on art and artifacts. The University of Oregon, established in 1872, held its first matriculation in 1876.

I was lucky in finding the Saturday Market in Eugene and marveled at the abilities and ingenuity of the many craftspeople and, the well-made items. Twig furniture made of green willow, ash, or alder was for sale by a local woman who gathered the branches from her farm near Creswell. One could find something of interest in all the many crafts represented. I am a basket picker-upper and came away with two reed baskets.

Since the beginning, Oregon has attracted rugged individualists whether it be in politics, personal life style, business, or education . . . those daring to accomplish. It was just such an individual who struck gold in the hills southeast of Cottage Grove . . . **James "Bohemia" Johnson** . . . in the 1890's. The story goes that Bohemia, an emigrant from Bohemia, killed an Indian and with another man hid in the Calapooya Mountains to prevent capture. The incident turned out great for Bohemia; he found high-quality gold. Unfortunately, the gold was on ledges which required mining by machinery so interest soon died out until 1891, when Dr. Oglesby opened the Champion and Noonday Mills at Music Ledge and for the next twenty years the mines yielded between five hundred thousand and a million dollars worth of high grade ore. When the milling ledges were exhausted, and they were down to low grade ore, the region was abandoned. However, each July old mining traditions are revived for the 4-day Bohemia Mining Days. The road is narrow, dirty, and extremely steep . . . I had rented a jeep at Cottage Grove as my car would never have made it. If you don't want to drive, there are tours out of Cottage Grove. One must use extreme care in walking through the mine areas as many of the old timbers could fall in or give way and overgrown bushes often hide the shafts. It is a part of Oregon not too many people visit but I found it definitely worth my time even though "narrow roads" are really not to my liking. It was a clear day and I could see the Pacific Ocean 130 miles distant. Pick up a travel guide or map at a nearby Chamber of Commerce, the Village Green or the National Forest Service Office for this journey.

Remember the **Goose** train ride that goes into the Bohemia Mining district (not as far as the mines). The locomotives are steam and diesel powered and it is a leisurely two and a half hour round trip into the foothills of the Calapooya Mountains and Bohemia's hiding place.

The trip to the mines had taken a time toll but back on I-5, I cruised a little faster and took the exit into Oakland about 18 miles north of Roseburg and at one time, an important transportation junction. Many of Oakland's old buildings are the same and still in active use. It is a small market town. Follow Oak Street east of town and inquire for the Carriage Works . . . they are makers of horse and pony driven rigs and are open daily. They have horses, mules, and ponies on the grounds. When finished, backtrack a little (get instructions from local residents) and you will be back on I-5 shortly.

At Sutherlin, one can depart for the coast cities of Reedsport or Winchester Bay. Five miles south of Roseburg is Winston, where just a few miles off the road you can take the family through the **Wildlife Safari**. This is a 600 acre drive-through animal park with three miles of graded trails. There are over 38 species of African and Asian animals, including lions, tigers, elephants, cheetahs, zebras, camels, ostriches, and birds of all kinds. There are a children's petting zoo, elephant rides, and sundown safari.

Steamboat is not a boat but a town, a tiny town . . . about 40 miles up the North Umpqua River on Highway 138 . . . then there is Steamboat Falls six miles on. Little Steamboat Creek is one of many moods . . . it can be roaring through a rock canyon, floating placidly between fern filled banks and overhanging tree branches, and the next moment find itself in another tantrum.

Note: to be "steamboated" means suckered by a slick promoter which is what happened many times when miners were slickered by a quick-witted shyster in overselling a worked-out mine or one that wasn't too prosperous. I wonder if that happened around Steamboat?

At Dry Creek, a few short miles east of Steamboat, is the grave of Bill Bradley. Bill lived here alone in the early 1900's, but one day, while trying to subdue a wild horse, he was fatally kicked. By the time professional help could get to him, he had died. Back of his grave is an Indian cave and the walls inside have many pictographs.

If you go far enough on this highway, you will be able to see the nine thousand foot plus peak of Mt. Thielsen reaching for the sky. You will also arrive at Diamond Lake in the heart of the Diamond Wilderness. It is an extremely popular resort for summer and winter sports in the Cascades.

Roseburg, sometimes called the timber capital of the nation, lies at the foot of the rugged timberland of the Cascade Mountains; its city sits on the edges of the North Umpqua River as it crashes, smashes, tumbles and topples its way to the ocean.

The county seat of Douglas County, Roseburg is always ready for a celebration . . . in February there is Storm Days at Reedsport, April the Wildflower Show at Glide, May the white water racing event at Glide, Daffodil Festival at Scottsburg . . . June, July, and August are filled with events and September culminates in the Melon Festival at Winston/Dillard and a Wine Festival in Roseburg.

There are vineyards at Melrose a few miles north of Roseburg and more at Tenmile a few miles south of Roseburg. Both are pleased to have visitors sample their wines and if conditions permit, take a tour.

Campgrounds, picnic areas, small exit roads, bicycle areas, fishing, boating, the list could go on and on . . . almost everything that a traveler could wish to do for outdoor recreation is available from Roseburg to the Oregon/California border. You almost stumble over places to go, things to see, and you are in a constant state of decision making.

Still on or having returned to I-5, the next stop is a **must.** Wolf Creek (Tavern) Inn. Originally it was called a tavern because that was a common name for 19th century roadside inns but actually liquor was not served until 1930. Wolf Creek Inn has a lot of firsts for important visitors . . . Ulysses S. Grant stopped when he was a Second Lt., President Rutherford B. Hayes and party stopped briefly and General Sherman dropped in for food and lodging. Sinclair Lewis called it home for a brief spell while writing a story; Joaquin Miller, Jack London, Clark Gable, and Herbert Hoover have walked through the doors of the oldest state hostelry and watering hole.

However, hundreds of just "I's" have visited this unique Tavern/Inn over the years from the horse and buggy days to grand touring cars and sexy Isuzu's. If you plan to stay in the summer, reservations should be made ahead of time as there are only eight rooms that can accommodate 16 guests. The food is simple and good and the premises are immaculate. While there, if one really wants to do some backcountry exploring, continue on to Galice but pick up a Forest Service map and get instructions before taking the trip.

Hidden among the tall timber between Roseburg and Grants Pass is a place called "Mexia's Pies". It is hard to get there or even see it driving south from Portland, but should you be going north to Portland, slow down and take the exit. A piece of her pie is a treat for the palate.

In the nearby area of Wolf Creek is Sunny Valley, and you will find the Grave Creek Covered Bridge with six windows on each side. As you drive down Coyote Creek Road, you will come to the ghost town of **Golden** where the deserted school, miner's cabin, church, general store and carriage shed still stand . . . deserted.

Grants Pass is a "pass-through" to well known attractions such as the Oregon Caves, the Redwoods, Crater Lake, Jacksonville, Oregon Shakespeare Festival and the Oregon Coast. It also hosts river guides that will take you on fishing outings, serene river floats, jet boat rides or whitewater rafting. Here, at the Riverside Motel, you can make arrangements to take the spectacular Hellgate Canyon trip through the lower Rogue which is one of the most remote and challenging water courses anywhere. You will see rock walls over 250 feet high and scenic beauty along the river banks including wild animals peeking at you from ashore, and birds, birds, birds who know it is really their territory, not yours. **Take it, you'll llove it!** I had taken the trip and became so excited watching everything around me, I forgot to take a single picture.

Grants Pass offers backpacking, hiking, hunting, horseracing, sightseeing, shopping, spelunking, goldpanning, golfing, water skiing or snow skiing or **just doing your own thing.**

Oregon's own . . . myrtlewood . . . there is a factory and showroom at 6th and "D" Streets in Grants Pass where handcrafted gifts of myrtlewood are made. I stopped, left considerable cash, but found something for almost everyone on my coming Christmas list.

Indian Mary Park out of Grants Pass is a lovely site to have a picnic, camp for a week, hold a family reunion, whatever.

I had never stopped to see the **Mint Farms** on Riverbanks Road in Grants Pass. I made up my mind to do so now. It is eight hundred acres of purple green mint set against the purple hills and blue waters of the Applegate River. Live white geese wasnder about at their pace as they are the "keepers" of the mint . . . they eliminate the fields of weeds and bugs.

Grants Pass "Oregon Cavemen" are the talk of the town. These fur-skin clad pranksters with their fang-like teeth, awesome headgear, and shaggy wigs are the good-will ambassadors-at-large for Josephine County. The Cavemen claim the marble halls of the Oregon Caves as their home and supposedly their food and drink consists of dinosaur meat and blood of saber tooth tigers.

Almost to Medford and the **Oregon Vortex**; I had stopped before and it was fascinating . . . I stopped again. It is also called the House of Mystery as it has very strange magnetic forces. John Lister opened the House in 1940. It is an old assay office that slid into its current awkward position. During the tour items appear to roll uphill, taller people appear shorter, visitors are asked to exchange places on level ground, or what appears to be level, and when they do so, their height changes by inches. The manager of the "strange house" says you may get some funny looking pictures because of the light change every 22.33 seconds. However, you are free to take as many pictures and poke about as you wish. There is a museum nearby with many old and interesting objects.

As you come down Blackwell Hill and drop into the beautiful Rogue River Valley, on a clear day, it is a sight to behold. No wonder the ballad Rogue River Valley became known internationally.

In 1854, the last major Indian battle was fought near Table

Rocks. By this time, travel was much easier and places more accessible for the pioneer. More than 2000 pack mules and 100 freight wagons were operating north and south carrying as much as $100,000 worth of gold dust to banks in Portland and San Francisco. Their route closely parallels that of today's I-5.

The Rogue River water, swirling, wild, leaping, calm, cavorting, uncontrolled, some parts of it accessible only by boat and guide, is widely known for its fine fishing of trout, steelhead, and salmon. People come from "all over the world" to "shoot the rapids" from Grants Pass to Gold Beach. The entire Rogue River pathway is majestic as it cuts its way through the Siskiyou Mountains, down canyons, and calm interludes to meet the restless waves at Gold Beach, Oregon.

Farmers were lured to the Rogue River Valley by the fertile soil and wonderful growing conditions as well as gold. But, when gold was found in Jacksonville in 1852 it not only brought in more miners but more farmers and businessmen.

When the Oregon/California (O&C) Railroad reached southern Oregon in 1883, Jacksonville refused to pay $25,000 for the privilege of having the railroad run through its vicinity and so the railroad built a station at Middleford on Bear Creek some ten miles west. Though "poor in purse" the people of Jackson County contributed generously to the building of the railroad. Many farmers subscribed quantities of wheat or other grain, beaver skins, and sawmill owners gave cross ties to be used in laying the track . . . many made direct cash payments.

It was time for other small cities lining the railroad route to stand up and be counted but Central Point refused to lend financial aid toward completion of the railroad through the southern part of the state. O&C couldn't leave it off the main line but for a number of years refused to stop at the town or to sell tickets to that destination.

Middleford eventually became Medford and the city became incorporated two years later. It didn't take long for it to grow both in size and importance and was soon considered a major shipping and railroad center. The county seat was moved to Medford in 1926. It is of interest to learn that the first order of business after incorporation, was to establish three ordinances . . . (1) against disorderly conduct, (2) minors loitering at the depot, and (3) hogs from running loose within the town.

86

It was time to give up for the day and this I did at the Red Lion Inn on N. Riverside in Medford. I was given a room overlooking Bear Creek and the large city park of Medford where I sat in the dusk and watched a softball game being played, listened to the trickling water as it glided on to the waiting, mighty Rogue River.

I slept a little late the next morning but started out for Jacksonville about 9:00 a.m. Students, residents, movie set workers, writers, tourists, locals roamed the streets, filled the shops, and thronged the Jacksonville Museum. A week's stay would be too short but I had three hours and planned to use every minute to the best advantage. The old Jackson County Courthouse now houses the historical museum and also the Southern Oregon Historical Society. It became a historic landmark in 1966.

I strolled through the city visiting all the antique shops and other specialty stores just for "the fun of it" and to "get a feel for the place". I looked in at the US Hotel on California Street which is now used for a local bank. I moved on to the Beekman Residence, McCully House, Nunan Mansion. The Nunan Mansion was the home of Jeremiah Nunan, wealthy merchant. Furnishings, woodwork, paneling, stained glass . . . all have been maintained or replaced with exact replicas. This also applies to most of the other historic homes in the area.

The Jacksonville Inn, built in 1863, has had extensive renovation and now has a gift shop featuring Oregon wines and Oregon gift products. They have a small hotel for guests and one of Jackson County's finest dining rooms in the basement . . . beautifully appointed.

About a mile out of Jacksonville returning west to Medford, I stopped at the Pioneer Village which is filled with pioneer history. More than twenty historic buildings have been relocated here and most are more than a 100 years old. It has one of the most extensive displays of horse drawn vehicles . . . prison wagon, hearse, steam tractor, and wagons used for making major movies in or near Jacksonville. There is also a miner's cabin, mine tunnel, mining equipment, jail, moonshiner's cabin and **train ride for the kids.** Part of the village has been remodeled into a nice dinner house. They also hold outdoor old-time melodramas on weekends during the summer to which tourists and home-folk flock.

Gold . . . 1852 . . . Miners throng to Jacksonville. So much mining was done under the streets of the city that some of the streets have actually given way. Others are held together with heavy underpinnings.

The Peter Britt Musical Festival is gaining great renown as professional musicians throughout the United States gather in Jacksonville to present classical concerts and recitals in August each year. Over a thousand listeners often attend each evening.

I was hungry but decided to move on . . . my stomach is pretty well clock-set to eating between 12:00 noon and 1:00 p.m. but sometimes it has to wait its turn.

I returned to Medford, took Highway 62 north to Eagle Point about 10 miles northeast of Medford on Little Butte Creek. Right on Main Street is the Butte Creek Mill established in 1872. This water powered grist mill is going for its 200 years of operation and still mills flour, cornmeal, cereals, and pancake mix on the old original stone buhrs. The buhrstones were quarried in France of quality quartz, are four feet in diameter, weigh about 1400 pounds, and were shipped around the Horn to get to Eagle Point, OR. The mill does not run on a water wheel, instead, a small dam takes water from the creek and carries it for a half mile into a canal called a millrace. This flows into a penstock below the mill where its weight provides enough pressure to turn the turbine and power the grinding machinery. The used water then goes out the tailrace and back into the creek. Observing how efficiently this works, it added to my admiration and respect for my forefathers and their "know-how". Visitors can watch the milling process and also watch the mill-owner, Peter Crandall. He gauges if all is going well by the strange noises emitted from within the mill.

I bought some stone ground flour and cereal. Mr. Crandall said their wheat came from Montana, rye from eastern Oregon and corn from central California because it was high quality and they settled for nothing less.

I stopped at the local store close-by, bought some bread, cheese, and a small bottle of wine, found my way to a park on Little Butte Creek a couple of blocks away, and among the huge, old shade trees, I enjoyed my European lunch, the day, and my company .

In the same direction, a few miles up the Rogue River out of Trail, OR., I came to Lost Creek Dam completed in 1973. Each year annual production credits the hatchery with almost 2,000,000 spring chinook, 206,000 coho, 100,000 summer steelhead, 460,000 winter steelhead, 168,000 rainbow legals, and 2,300,000 rainbow and kokanee fingerlings or about 5 million fish. Fishermen and women love to hear those figures and no wonder one can hardly find a "rock" to call one's own along the Rogue River during fishing season.

Old Timer's Story . . . Ed Shieffelin, one of the first to try for gold in Jacksonville but one of the unlucky in not finding it, moved on to Arizona and eventually founded Tombstone, AZ., after striking it rich. He returned to Oregon a rich man but he still had "gold fever" and started prospecting in the Tiller/Trail area. He was found dead, apparently of natural causes, and alongside him were deposits of very rich gold ore. There were no clues as to where the gold had been found but his famed red blanket was missing. It is surmised that he left the red blanket wherever the rich gold samples came from. This is the mystery of the Lost Red Blanket Mine.

Going on to the north in this direction, one can get to Fish Lake, Lake of the Woods, Howard Prairie, Hyatt Lake, take a drive through the Rogue River National Forest, and picnic at any one of hundreds of places along the way. The trip is a kaleidoscope of specatacular views especially of Mt. McLoughlin with its nose 9,450 feet in the air and often snow-capped until July or August.

I stopped for a cup of coffee at a restaurant in Shady Cove and a "native" told me the story of "One-eyed Charlie Parkhurst". Old stage coach drivers earned good or bad reputations for evading or outwitting ambushes by bandits and the drivers were considered a pretty rugged bunch . . . one of the toughest for years was One-eyed Charlie. It was only upon the death of Charlie in 1879 that Charlie was found to be Charlotte Parkhurst.

Ashland, 12 miles south of Medford, was to be my destination for the evening. I checked into the elegant, tastefully appointed Ashland Hills Inn directly off I-5, second exit south. The view is harmonious with nature's setting in every direction. I rested briefly and drove to the Ashland Chamber of Commerce, downtown, and picked up their valuable and informative brochures on Ashland and the surrounding area.

In Lithia Plaza are two water fountains . . . one contains Lithia water which, it is said, if taken in the proper amounts, will make one feel like a colt again. The minerals in it give it a very strange taste.

Nearby is Lithia Park placed in a gorgeous natural setting in a canyon with a natural stream running its full length. Mr. John McLarin, who designed the Golden Gate Park in San Francisco, also played a part in landscaping Lithia. I dallied, and dallied, and dallied. The park would be a credit to a large city and it was filled with travelers and residents enjoying everything from picnics, watching graceful swans floating on the man-made lakes, to tennis enthusiasts practicing their techniques.

I purchased tickets for the Elizabethan Stage for the evening (*Richard III*), the Black Swan Theatre for the following afternoon, and a showing of "*What the Butler Saw*" in the Angus Bowmer Theatre for the following evening. The Oregon Shakespearean Festival has grown from a small event to an eight month season of plays in three theatres.

The Tudor Guild Shop of the Oregon Shakespearean Festival Association sells costumes that are no longer needed by the theatre. Many downtown businesses have turned building facades into old English copies and many of the old buildings have been preserved.

I learned the community of Ashland began in 1852 with a water powered sawmill. During the next year a flour grist mill was erected and in 1868, the industrial efforts were expanded to include a woolen mill. Because of the manufacturing nature of its beginning the Post Office officially carried the name as Ashland Mills until 1871 when it dropped the Mills designation. The town was called Ashland by the populace supposedly after Ashland, Ohio, but there is another faction who said it was named after Ashland, Virginia. Take your choice.

Mt. Ashland was another **must.** I wanted to see the ski resort as well as the view. Wild flowers now covered the winter snowcapped slopes. Ski facilities are open Thanksgiving through April . . . there is a lodge, rental shop, beginning and advanced slopes and cross country trails. Chairlifts and surface lifts provide access to 22 runs. The drive took about an hour. On my way back to Ashland, I stopped at a well recommended restaurant . . . Callahan's Lodge which is practically across from the Ashland Ski Road exit. It is a quaint, clean, outstanding Italian and American food restaurant and my veal scallopini was extraordinary.

I arrived back in Ashland, parked the car near the theatre, took a leisurely walk through more quaint shops. I returned to the outdoor theatre in time to watch the costumed dancers and troubadours singing and dancing 17th century London

90

style.

It was about 11:3Q p.m., when the play ended and I was glad I had brought along a warm jacket. Upon retiring, I decided to stay one more day . . . one more day in this superb state of Oregon. It would be a lazy day, a day of absorbing what I had seen and done and heard. I reflected that in my travels I had been so very fortunate. I did not have to worry about Indians attacking me, freezing or getting heat stroke riding in a covered wagon. Instead, I could go to almost any scenic spot of history or recreational area within minutes or hours, travel down an interstate highway in a modern car, covering hundreds of miles a day, talk to numerous people, choose among hundreds of motels, hotels, inns, restaurants, and shops of all kinds . . . if only I could bring my greatgrandmother back over the same route she traveled at 25.

I had completed most of the things I had planned for this trip and made notes of what I wanted to do and see the next time. I would be going over the Siskiyou Mountains the day after tomorrow and down into California, continuing into the **State of Jefferson.** My last questioning thought before falling asleep was "Where did the name Siskiyou Mountains come from?"

I learned the word "Siskiyous" is the Indian word for "bob-tailed". In 1828, Alexander McLeod, a Hudson Bay trapper, was heading a party in the mountains; they were lost in a snowstorm, suffered severe privations and lost several horses, among them the **bob-tailed** horse belonging to the leader. This mountain pass was thereafter called "the Pass of the Siskiyou" a name that was later given the whole range.

Note: Valley View Vineyards out of Jacksonville in the Applegate Valley is open for tasting, sales and informal tours in the summer from 11-5 everyday and 1-5 on weekends in the winter.

Another **must** of the many in Southern Oregon is a visit to Harry and David's Bear Creek Orchards and their Country Store. In business since 1936, their "goodies" are known throughout the world. This stop alone will take an hour . . . in fact, you may do all your gift buying for the coming year while there and still have time for a bite to eat in their quaint, immaculate restaurant.

INDEX

Addendum From Grants Pass to Crescent City, CA

Wilderville
Wonder
Selma
Kerby
Cave Junction
Oregon Caves
Oregon Caves Chateau
Hayes Hill
Patrick Creek Lodge

Addendum . . . State of Jefferson

History

This area originally was bordered on the west by the Pacific Ocean north to a lateral line about in the area of Eugene, Oregon; south laterally a little south of Red Bluff, CA. The eastern edge ran from near Brothers, Oregon; Lakeview, Alturas, CA and around Indian Falls, CA.

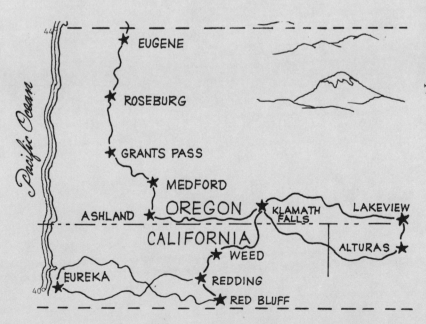

NOTES:

Addendum from Grants Pass to Crescent City, CA; Brookings, OR

A few more passing words on Grants Pass . . . the town first came into being as a stopping place on the California Stage route. But, one day a messenger came riding into town with the exciting news that General Grant had captured Vicksburg and the city was called Grants Pass to celebrate the occassion.

For the traveler who is taking Hwy. 199 out of Grants Pass to the Oregon or Calfiornia coast there are many beautiful recreational areas to stop and see, stay over-night, or for a month; as well as a wealth of historical sports and national history.

Wilderville will be one of the first of the small towns you pass. It was first called Slate Creek but was later changed and renamed after its first Postmaster, Joseph L. Wilder. The little hamlet sits at the door of a narrow valley that extends to the Calfifornia line.

Wonder comes along next and it is said it was named by settlers who "wondered" how a merchant who established a store at this place would ever hope to survive. Even driving under 55 mph, you pass through both of these communities so quickly you have to keep a sharp, quick eye open so as not to miss them.

Selma was mainly a settlement of miners who took a good supply of ore out of the surrounding mountains and many early gold strikes were made in this vicinity.

Kerby was a larger town and an important trading center and placer mining camp during the gold rush. In 1858, it was a town of tents and shacks known as Kerbyville. However, from the once thriving settlement of some 500 population, it has faded into oblivion as the rich placer mines were worked out. The Kerbyville Museum is located on Highway 199 in the heart of Kerby. The house is one of the oldest in the town. It was the county seat for many years. It is open every day, May through October . . . no admission, and well worth one's time, of probably 30 minutes, to stop and browse in the museum and walk around the once thriving little town.

A few miles north of Cave Junction, you will come to the Woodland Deer Park. Both adult and child will find it a **must**. They can hand feed the some five different kinds of foreign deer and take pictures to their heart's content. Mother Goose Land, picnic tables and refreshments (souvenirs) are available. There is an admission charge.

Cave Junction was named because it is the junction that one takes to the Oregon Caves. This is a good place to stop for taking care of your old friend "the car" and "yourself". There are several good restaurants, lounges, and interesting shops for browsing including antiques, crafts, and modern items.

The **Oregon Caves** was proclaimed a national monument in 1909 some 35 years after it was discovered by Elijah ~~Bristow~~, a pioneer, who "lucked out" in finding it while chasing a bear that disappeared into the mountainside. The Caves are called the Marble Halls of Oregon in the Elijah Mountain . . . they are limestone and marble formations in the Siskiyou range. The Caves contain chambers, corridors, and passageways of incredible beauty brought about by the ceaseless flow of water in subterranean darkness. Fluted columns and pillars rise along the passages and colored lights placed at intervals give the marble walls a blue cast. More than 50 points of interest are contained within these caves . . . **Niagara Falls**, a waterfall frozen eternally into marble, **Queen's Organ** is a room that gives out musical sounds and as you go deeper you come to **Paradise Lost**, a high-walled chamber covered, in what appears to be pendants of crystal chandeliers. **Joaquin Miller's Chapel** is a vast cathedral-like room, named for the poet, who visited in 1907. **Dantes Inferno** is a huge chasm where marble, under crimson lights, resembles the inside of a seething cauldron.

The Caves Chateau consists of six stories where one can arrange to stay overnight in modern, clean accommodations. There is a fine dining room, souvenir shop, and outside benches to accommodate those who want to relax and take in the beauty of this wonderland visually.

The Oregon Caves Game Refuge surrounds the caves and teems with wildlife of all kinds. Oftentimes, the bear and deer, who have become quite tame, will look at you quizzically at close range . . . are you friend or foe?

As you pass over Hayes Hill going south (or north) which sits on the corner of the Siskiyou National Forest, you will see the graceful madrona tree. It changes during the seasons, but if you are fortunate, you may catch it when its leaves are dark green, the bark is smooth, it is covered in waxy white blossoms and scarlet fruit.

The opportunities for exercise, relaxation, fun, discovery, history lessons, are legion in this area. Plant and animal life of

96

all kinds roam and grow amid the various forest types and climates. If man treats nature kindly, uses only what he needs, is reverent of what has been given him, Nature will see that there is always a renewal for his enjoyment.

As the tourist reaches the coast Highway 101, he has a choice of going north to Oregon via Brookings (Ship Ashore/Smith River, CA), or south to Crescent City/Eureka, CA. *See Guide One for this trip and also Patrick Creek Lodge.*

Some of the material taken for the addendum on State of Jefferson is from the book of State of Jefferson by Jack Sutton ©1965. Reprinted with permission by the Josephine County Historical Society, Grants Pass, OR.

While dates can drive us crazy, sometimes they are necessary for continuity. In 1803, Jefferson State actually became a territory of the United States as a result of the Louisiana Purchase. Later, two great states . . . Oregon and California . . . gobbled up the area and each settled for half. But, since then the region has periodically seethed with rebellion when Jeffersonites on both sides of the border felt neglected by state and federal governments particularly in the distribution of highway funds and post office considerations . . . usually with good reason.

The first rebellion was quite serious when in 1852, California demanded a new state of **Shasta**. In 1854, agitation began again when southern Oregon argued for a state of Jackson, but Oregon was given statehood in 1859 and the subject was temporarily put on ice.

In 1935, the State of Jefferson was brought to the fore when John L. Childs of Crescent City, CA., got himself elected governor by a number of constituents and put on a mock serious campaign for statehood. His promotion of the separate state was so successful, it was given credit for achieving great improvements in transportation facilities in northern California.

In 1941, the people of Yreka drew national attention by setting up road blocks across US Highway 99 and collecting tolls from travelers crossing the state line. This group created the **Great Seal of the State of Jefferson**. The Seal is a gold pan with XX painted on the bottom which was to symbolize Jeffersonians being doublecrossed by politicians in both states. Cave Junction, OR., and Dunsmuir, CA., threatened to secede and take the State of Shasta with them. Believe it or not, quick action by state legislatures mollified the unhappy people.

97

However, it is believed that the State of Jefferson is more a state of mind than actuality. It is agreed that it is a state of Nature's own division . . . geographically, topographically, and emotionally . . . it is a country by itself. It is self sufficient. Its boundaries contain water, fish, wildlife, farm and orchard land as well as forest and mineral resources to exist on its own. The boundaries originally stretched from the Pacific Ocean on the west coast to a point in the high plateau country around Lakeview, OR., and Alturas, CA., on the east. The north boundary, gave the 44th parallel around Eugene, Springfield, Oregon, and the south boundary the 40th parallel which would run approximately around Garberville, Red Bluff, and Indian Falls, CA.

A newspaper is still being published out of Alturas, CA., called "State of Jefferson".

The country we have visited in these **Guides** included this Jefferson territory. No one would question the courage of the great pioneers who migrated to the land nor the hardihood of those who survived. They were certainly a generation of hard workers, adventurers, daring, bold, and met the challenges of life's vicissitudes with little complaint.

Often the men lived lonely and dangerous lives and sowed their seed from Port Orford on the southern Oregon coast to the Wallowa foothills. Some were pillars of rectitude who married early, begot large families, and grew gaunt and gray and old in sober monogamy. Others punished their livers with bad whiskey and pursued their loves in the Indian lodges as well as in the brothels of Pendleton and settlements of Klamath Basin. They were audacious, brave and courageous . . . and I wonder . . . men were measured by different standards then . . . would they have wanted it any different?

We of today complain of **stress** and we must get away. When we do, let us look and remember the recreational and national legacy **they** left us for releasing **our stress**.

YOUNG PEOPLE'S GUIDE

Exciting, thrilling, hair-raising, spine-tingling places to see. Your maps follow the routes taken in the first Ten Guides. Fill in names and places you want to stop.

My personal Travel Genie's name is _____.

The two mascot's names are _____ **and** _____.

Granddaughter Krista Foster says, "My mom and dad like the game where you have to keep quiet and not say anything until you come to a certain town or gas station. My parents like that game best especially at the end of the day."

MY NAME _____

YOUR NAME _____

JEFF

JEFF   SONJA

NOTES:

Name your **Travel Genie**

Young People's Special Travel Treat Index

Guide 1   Eureka . . . . zoo and playground
Crescent City . . . . tetrapods
Klamath, CA . . . . Trees of Mystery
Avenue of Giants . . . . Redwood Trees
Ship Ashore Pirates Den

Guide 2   Port Orford . . . . Game Park on Highway
Prehistoric Rain Garden
Sea Lion Caves . . . . look for guillemot bird
(there is a black Guillemot and a foolish guillemot)
Darlingtonia . . . . plants that eat insects
Sand Lake . . . . ride dune buggies
Newport . . . . . . Undersea Gardens and Wax Museum
Florence . . . . Indian Forest
Lincoln City area . . . . Devil's Lake

Guide 3   Lincoln City area . . . . Lacey's Dollhouse
Pixieland
Astoria . . . . Column and Maritime Museum
Westport ferry
Multnomah Falls
Bonneville Dam . . . . children's playground
The Dalles . . . . red, white and blue train

Guide 4   Prineville . . . . Bicentennial bike route
Bend area . . . . Reindeer Ranch
Peterson Rock Garden
Arnold Ice Caves
Three Sisters . . . . wagon rides
Feed llamas at Peterson's llama ranch
Children's Pet Parade at Harvest time
Fort Klamath . . . . Mare's eggs

Guide 5   Klamath Lake . . . . Pelicans
Lava Beds . . . . . . Cindercones, Skull Cave, Merrill Ice
Cave, Captain Jack's Stronghold
Bly
Grizzly Bear Peak
Lost Forest
Goose Lake . . . . disappearing lake
Fairport

Guide 6   Lakeview area . . . . Rabbit and Coyote Hills
Hart Mountain nodules . . . . fire opal, sunstones
. . . . petrified wood
Shasta Dam . . . . water ports, houseboats
Mt. Shasta . . . . Ski area

Dunsmuir . railroad town, remains of old roundhouse
Dunsmuir area . . . . Redbud bush or "Judas Tree"
Redding Mall . . . . planetarium

Guide 7   Shasta Caverns
          Whiskeytown Lake
          Weaverville . . . . Chinese Temple
          Trinity Alps . . . . Sasquatch country, "Bigfoot"
          Eureka . . . . Samoa cookhouse
          Ferndale . . . . Gumdrop trees
          Super Skunk Train . . . . (Ft. Bragg—Willets)

Guide 8   Portland (only a few of the many places to visit)
          Children's Museum . . . 3037 SW 2nd—admission free
          Washington Park Zoo
          The Portland area has so many places to go and things
          to see for all the family; contact the Chamber of
          Commerce or Oregon Tourist Bureau for maps and
          sites of interest. There is the Jantzen Beach Shopping
          Center for children and a railcruise through the
          Columbia Gorge.

Guide 9   Portland to Eugene area
          Oregon State Fairgrounds
          Aurora Ox Barn Museum
          Champoeg State Park
          Salem . . . . State Capitol building and mall
          Salem Mill Creek . . . . . . fishing for children in season
          Enchanted Forest
          Ferries crossing Willamette River . . . . Eugene
          Eugene . . . . canoeing

Guide 10 Village Green . . . . Goose Train
          Oakland . . . . Carriage Works
          Winston . . . . Wildlife Safari
          Wolf Creek Tavern
          Indian Mary Park
          Oregon Vortex
          Jacksonville . . . . Pioneer Village and train rides
          Butte Creek Mill
          Lost Creek Dam . . . . Applegate Dam
          Ashland Park . . . . Shakespearean plays
          Oregon Caves
          Woodland Deer Park
          Grants Pass Mint Farm

***Watch for concrete bridges on Hwy. 101 and see if you can
count 17 from southern Oregon border to Astoria???**

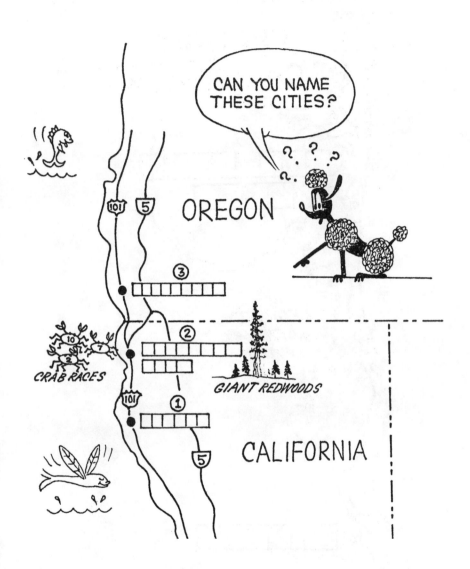

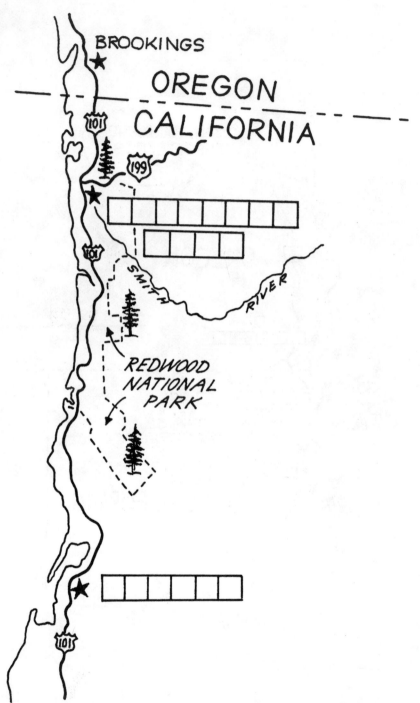

Guide 1

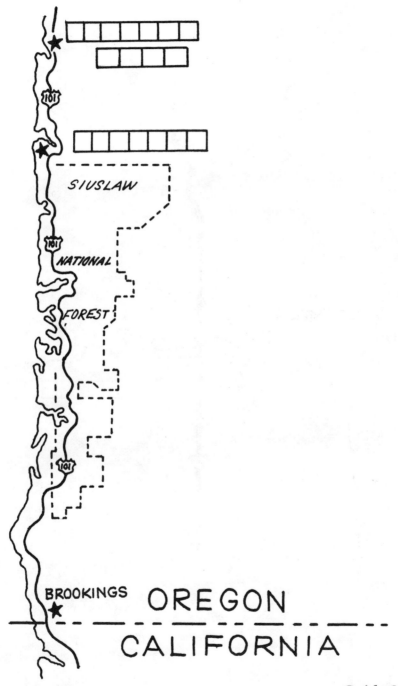

SIUSLAW

NATIONAL

FOREST

BROOKINGS

OREGON

CALIFORNIA

Guide 2

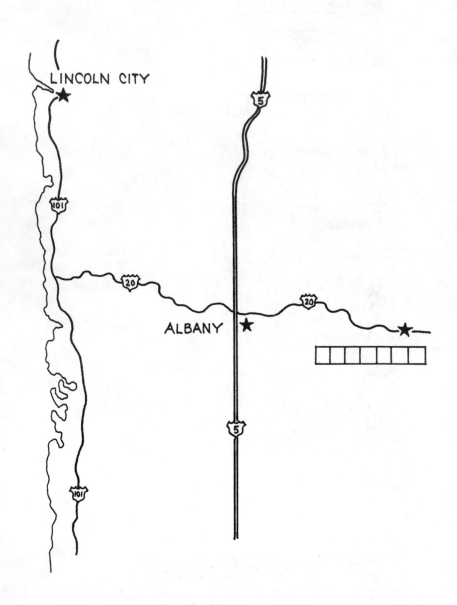

Guide 3

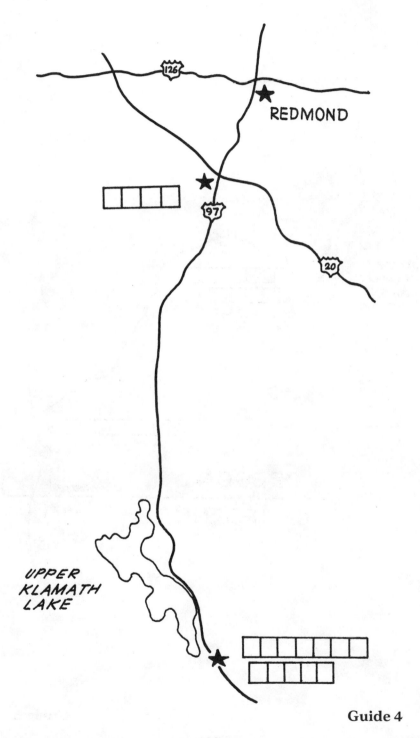

REDMOND

126

97

20

UPPER
KLAMATH
LAKE

Guide 4

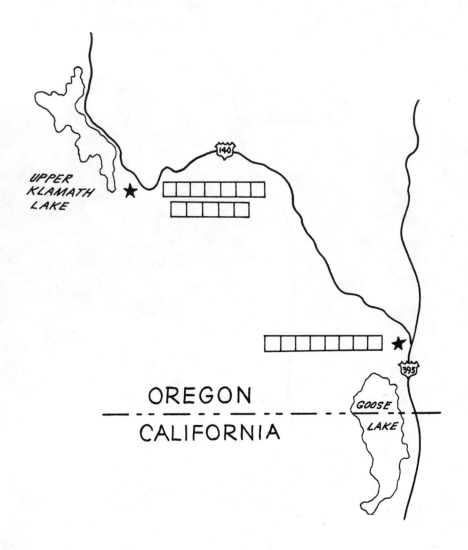

UPPER
KLAMATH
LAKE

OREGON

CALIFORNIA

GOOSE
LAKE

Guide 5

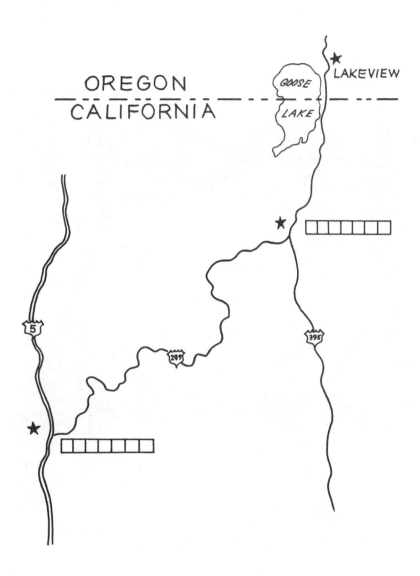

OREGON

CALIFORNIA

GOOSE LAKE

★ LAKEVIEW

★ ☐☐☐☐☐☐

5

299

395

★ ☐☐☐☐☐☐☐

Guide 6

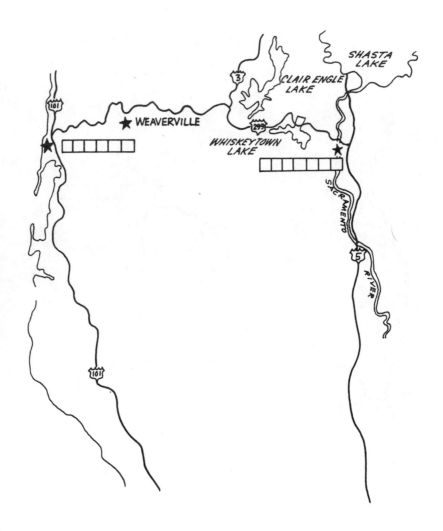

SHASTA LAKE

CLAIR ENGLE LAKE

WEAVERVILLE

WHISKEYTOWN LAKE

SACRAMENTO RIVER

Guide 7

112

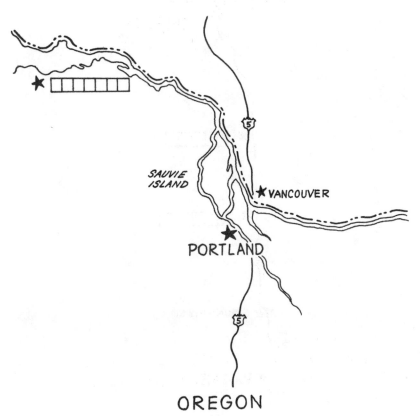

WASHINGTON

SAUVIE
ISLAND

★VANCOUVER

PORTLAND

OREGON

Guide 8

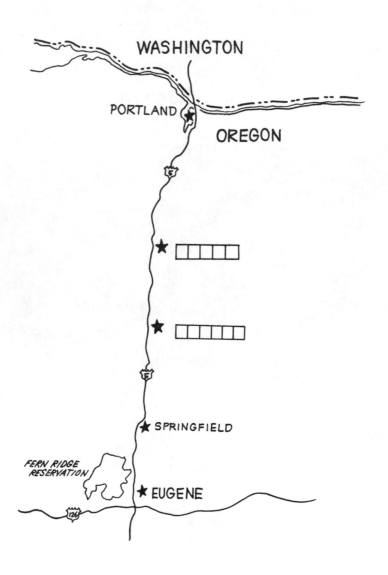

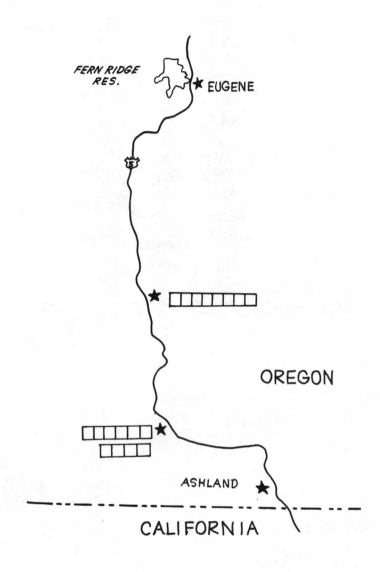

FERN RIDGE RES.

★ EUGENE

5

OREGON

ASHLAND ★

CALIFORNIA

Guide 10

Redwood _____ in _____

Battery Point Lighthouse   Crescent City, CA

Name Me _____

I am _____
Patrick's Creek Inn, Oregon

Crescent City, _____

Rekwai . . . Yurok Indian Home
In California _____ **or Oregon** _____?

Full speed ahead at _____Oregon

Prehistoric _____Garden, _____Highway

Gui _____ **Bird** . . . . **Sea Lion Caves**

Sea Lions at _____

120

CLOMP!

The plants at _____ eat bugs.

Sand buggy at sand dunes on

the _____ Coast

Lacey's Dollhouse at_____City, Oregon

Haystack Rock _____**Oregon**

Ferries at_____Oregon
_____Oregon
_____Oregon

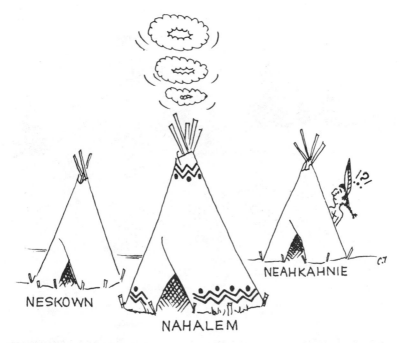

NESKOWN

NAHALEM

NEAHKAHNIE

Where did you find me? _____

Tillamook Burn at _____, **Oregon**

Cascade Locks . . . I am on the _____**River in Oregon?**

Devil's Lake in_____

Arch _____

Buried treasure

Three Sister mountains at _____**Oregon**

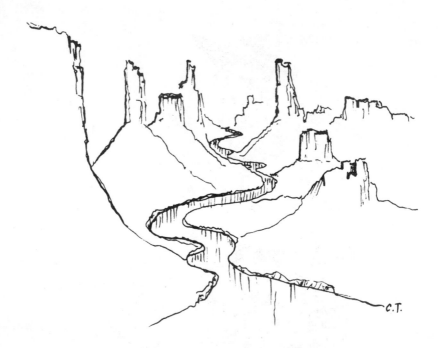

I am called the _____**River . . . Redmond**

River that runs backwards _____Klamath Area

_____Eggs . . . Fort Klamath, Oregon

_____Cave . . . . .Lava Beds

Rabbit Hill/Coyote Hill
We live at _____ **View, Oregon**

Goose Lake . . . . **Lake that wasn't there**
This lake is in both the States of _____ **and** _____

Sonja at Blizzard_____

_____Tailed deer   found_____

Shasta _____water _____in California

Whiskeytown Lake at _____California

Old Chinese Temple at _____California

Samoa Cookhouse " _____ house-reach"

Super Skunk Train
I run from _____ to _____ in California

Old Skunk Trains use to _____

Hurry, don't miss Portland Tri _____

Portland, Oregon . . . City of _____ ____

_____ capital of Oregon

Enchanted _____, out of _____

We are canoeing at _____, Oregon

Indian _____ Park

Wolf Creek Tavern at _____, Oregon

Grants Pass _____**men**

Ashland _____**plays**

Woodland Deer Park in_____**Oregon**

What is my name_____? Where do I live_____?

SPECIAL NOTES AND INFORMATION

Tourist Travel Treats Oregon/Northern California
Author . . . . Wynne Gibson
Illustrator . . . . Charles Travers

MAPS: _____

MOTELS/INNS: _____

RESTAURANTS: _____

RECREATIONAL FACILITIES: _____

PLACES TO SEE: _____

NOTES: _____